RED IS DEMOCRAT

RED IS DEMOCRAT

DANIEL ALAN BRUBAKER

First Think And Tell paperback edition 2023

10 9 8 7 6 5 4 3 2 1

Library of Congress Cataloguing-in-Publication Data

Brubaker, Daniel A., 1970-

Red is Democrat

1. United States—Politics and government—Philosophy. 2. United States—Moral conditions. 3. Social values—United States. 4. National characteristics—American. 5. Racism—United States. 6. United States—History. I. Title.

ISBN 978-1-949-12301-2

For my children

and yours

CONTENTS

PREFACE

As the United States faced their greatest internal battle yet, over the moral question of slavery, President Abraham Lincoln famously said, "A house divided against itself cannot stand." Was Lincoln asserting that everyone should just "get along" and "agree to disagree"? Absolutely not! Justice denied to men and women subjected to involuntary servitude demanded a righteous answer. It would have been wrong to say that the enslavers were only embracing "their truth."

Americans today are again arrayed for the same war. On one side are those who insist, like Lincoln, that truth exists apart from individual preference, and that justice is not mere social construct. On the other side, just as before, stand the Democrats.

I know some kind, fair-minded, moral, and compassionate people who are Democrats. Perhaps you do, too. What baffles me is *why they are Democrats*.

What could cause good and decent[1] people to do, or support, bad things? My personal alarm at the advance of the totalitarian mindset, open depravity—indeed, apparent wholesale abandon of reason and virtue—on the left side of the American political landscape today (with the evident approval of a major proportion of Americans) prompted me to write this book.

Why, I asked myself, would *any* decent person support the Democratic Party, an entity that:

- systemically judges people by the color of their skin or other unchosen traits
- rejects science and reason
- suppresses dissent
- calls good evil and evil good
- approves and encourages the physical and emotional harm of children
- encourages theft and supports slavery
- rejects the very notion of objective truth
- openly celebrates immorality and mocks virtue
- excuses, advocates, and even propagates lawlessness and violence
- treats immigrants and members of certain ethnic groups as subhuman
- scorns America's good core principles such as liberty and justice for all
- endorses fascism, undermines American self rule, and prefers a centralized global government often hostile to human rights and basic justice?

A political party like the one described above *can* exist in the United States, because we are a free country with a First Amendment that protects all kinds of speech and the expression of any opinion. However, such a party should not be a major force on the political landscape of any moral and decent society. Those who support such a party could hardly be seen as aspiring to morality or decency—unless they were to hold a distorted view of what those words mean.

Yet, not only does such a political party, the Democratic, exist in the United States—it is supported by greater than 100 million Americans, dominates the national media and academia, and recently held control of both Houses of Congress and (albeit illegitimately; see my book *By The People?*[2]) of the White House. Unless its supporters imagine the party to be different than it really is, something has once again gone gravely wrong in the hearts of many Americans.

Actually, I do not believe that a majority of Americans embrace the principles of the Democratic Party. Most Democrat voters do not want to do bad things. Rather, they have been sold shares in a Democrat slave plantation that hides behind a veneer of respectability bolstered by clever marketing and insider control of the institutions that shape public opinion.

I sense that many regular Democrat voters simply do not realize that the core principles of the Party never changed after slavery ended. Once they understand this, I believe many will abandon it, because that is not who we aspire to be as Americans.

Although many lack self-awareness, I am not alone in my basic assertions about the Democratic Party's nature. There are those who woke up even while wearing the Democrat label. Ronald Reagan was one example. More recently, read the words of former Hawaii congresswoman Tulsi Gabbard, a contender for the Democratic presidential nomination in 2020, announcing her departure:

I can no longer remain in today's Democratic Party, that's under the complete control of an elitist cabal of warmongers who are driven by cowardly wokeness, who divide us by racializing every issue, and stoking anti-white racism, who actively undermine our God-given freedoms that are enshrined in our Constitution, who are hostile to people of faith and spirituality, who demonize the police but protect criminals at the expense of law-abiding Americans, who believe in open borders, who weaponize the national security state to go after their political opponents, and—above all—who are dragging us ever closer to nuclear war. Now, I believe in a government that's of the people, by the people, and for the people. Unfortunately, today's Democratic Party does not. Instead, it stands for a government that is of, by, and for the powerful elite. I'm calling on my fellow common-sense, independent-minded Democrats to join me in leaving the Democratic Party.[3]

Now, I believe Democrats' greatest racism, by far, is directed against "black and brown" people and not against "white" people as Gabbard suggests (I place all these terms inside quotation marks since we are all varying shades of tan), and will discuss it in Chapter 1. And, my criticism of the Democratic Party goes well beyond Gabbard's. For now, I just note that even insiders see Democrats' assault on goodness, justice, and human decency.

Two Kinds of Democrats

I was recently talking with a new friend who identifies as a Democrat. I don't think she'd had many real conversations with someone critical of the Democratic Party, and she expressed surprise upon hearing that one of my core concerns is racism. She seemed even more startled to hear that its open embrace of racism is one of the basic reasons I find the Democratic Party unacceptable and could not bring myself to vote for or donate to a candidate flying the Democrat banner. She had come to the belief that the Democratic Party opposes racism, and it seemed to me as though she never had considered otherwise.

Many regular Democrat voters do not seem to think they are supporting a racist, bigoted, anti-science, cruel, and unjust party. True, elected Democrats' increasing smuttiness on moral issues makes some supporters uneasy, but Democrat voters tolerate the party's sleaze and obscenity because they have been led to believe that the Party supports science, opposes racism, advocates for justice and fairness, and so forth. Democratic operatives have done a remarkable job of distorting reality and maintaining this deception via a propaganda machine that now dominates the nation's (and to a large extent, the world's) cultural, educational, and governmental institutions, often at taxpayer expense and frequently via illegal or unethical maneuvers.

It is not my goal to alienate Americans who have long identified as Democrat. I want to persuade you that the cause of justice, science, opportunity for all, transparency, public safety and security, social responsibility, and compassion is better served if you withhold support from a political party that works against you at every turn on these points. I ask you to *reconsider your alliances*. I hope to win you away from a party unworthy of your allegiance. The Democratic Party should reform itself or be left a shell whose only supporters are the lechers and moral reprobates who actually subscribe to its anti-intellectual, immoral, and unjust agenda. Calling oneself a Democrat in the United States ought to carry a stigma.

In other words, this book is an attempt to make it uncomfortable to embrace the Democrat label. If you love all people, hate racism, believe in right and wrong, yearn for justice, and want opportunity for all, the Democratic Party is not your home, and it never was. It does not deserve you, because it does not align with any of your core principles.

Concerning Civility

Conversations across political divides these days often descend into name-calling and personal attack, serving no purpose for either side except to make each feel vindicated in their position and superior to the other. I am not interested in merely scoring points or taking cheap shots. This book, though frank, is an effort at peacemaking. Romans 12:8 says, "If possible, so far as it depends on you, be at peace with all men."

I am not against you, but rather corrupt principles and the leaders who work to advance them. Those are bad people. If you today call yourself a Democrat, I offer you an honest outside perspective. I am handing you a mirror.

Is the Republican Party the Answer?

This book is a reflection upon the two major U.S. political parties, with a focus of attention upon one of them, the Democratic. It is reasonable for readers to expect that the other party, the Republican, presents a contrast, as it ought. I do not argue that Republicans are angels. But there has always been a basic difference between the two parties. First, the Republican Party does not advance racism in its platform or policies. Nor does it oppose science. Nor does it sacrifice children at the altar of its political goals. Nor does it celebrate immorality. Nor does it advocate violence. Nor does it agitate for unequal application of laws. In virtually every way the Republican Party in its core stated principles and their underlying purpose is the opposite of the Democrat Party.

Many have recently observed that career insiders of the Republican Party often talk a good line but support Democrat priorities when they believe no one is looking. It is a serious problem, and the epithet "uniparty" fits such people. In truth, there are factions within the parties, but compromise of principles for tactical purposes is a dangerous game. The emergence of the Tea Party movement in 2009 was a principled response to what many Americans saw as betrayal of principles by Republican insiders.

While I believe parties serve an important function in rallying people around a set of principles, political partisanship is not the ultimate answer to our problems. I urge readers to consider the principles and the moral assertions discussed in the following pages. My objective is a sharpened common commitment to what is true and good and a clear rejection of that which is not.

So, this book is indeed a general rejection of the American Democratic Party, and a general affirmation of the *stated principles* of the Republican Party. While I urge readers to volunteer and become involved, I recommend vigilance with respect to the national Republican Party (RNC), the National Republican Congressional Committee (NRCC) or the National Republican Senatorial Committee (NRSC). My policy for nearly twenty years has been generous support for individual Republicans who are proven, or—in the case of untested candidates—seem solid, in their support of the good stated principles of the Republican Party. While it requires more work, such intentionality better fits the type of engaged self governance that we were all given as a heritage and should be careful not to squander.

I believe that Democrats have set up straw men that they call Republican, that look nothing like the actual Republican Party, its positions and policy priorities. But, this book is not principally about Republicans. It is about the Democratic Party, what it has been throughout its history, and what it remains today.

Reform Unlikely

What becomes of the Democrat Party is not my concern; it is the business of the Party and its voters. If Democrats can correct course and disavow racism, violence, immorality, rejection of science, hate, and the fascist impulse, they could become worthy, perhaps for the first time, of America, and worthy of the support of her citizens.

In order to illustrate my points throughout this book, it will be necessary to deal with the words and actions of specific individuals. I've chosen examples, but do not mean to suggest that any given person perfectly reflects the views or opinions of every single Democrat. I do believe that they tend to align with the Party's principles.

Most importantly, I propose that voting for Democrats, donating to Democratic candidates, or supporting the Democratic Party today carries with it some basic and implicit assumptions. The Party has a platform, this platform in my assessment is racist, immoral, unjust, authoritarian, and hateful. Voting for a Democrat running under that banner, or donating to that candidate or their Party equates to support for that platform which has very few (if any) redeeming qualities. While those holding office will change in time, I expect the core principles upon which the Democratic Party rests to persist. I hope they correct course, but their remarkable stability along the same path for more than two hundred years leaves me faint hope of any major change.

One Nation, Under God

I write as a voice of conscience. I do not set out to be anyone's enemy. The Bible says "Love must be sincere. Hate what is evil. Cling to what is good." Notice that this affirms that hate is good when its object is evil itself. The Bible does not direct us to hate *people*. Why is it a good thing to hate what is evil? For one thing, evil harms people. God loves people, and therefore hates what harms them. So should we.

It is a good thing when someone cares enough to show us our faults in love. In the 10th century BC, King Solomon praised the act of telling the truth in such a way when he said, "Faithful are the wounds of a friend, but deceitful are the kisses of an enemy." (Proverbs 27:6) A friend does not withhold criticism when criticism is needed. Indeed, flattery when criticism is warranted can be itself an act of hate.

My concern is for people. You are my brother or my sister. I want good for you, that all kinds of people may join with renewed clarity around serious problems.

I don't write for approval from those who already agree with me. Nor do I want to merely hasten the self-sorting of Americans into Democrat and Republican identity groups. I want to persuade across a divide. Music to my ears would be the words, "You know, I never thought about things that way before, and your book helped me to see more clearly. Thank you."

Perspectives

I'm 52 years old and have lived around the United States and the world. Some of your experiences are similar to mine, and some are different. But if you've also lived in the United States, we'll have both known a nation that was founded about 250 years ago on a set of propositions that included the bold statement that "We hold these truths to be self-evident, that all men are created equal and are endowed by their Creator with certain unalienable rights, that among these rights are Life, Liberty, and the pursuit of Happiness."

That it took a little more than 89 years to move as a nation toward the fuller realization of these principles, for example with the abolition of our national pre-existing condition of slavery, and though we still have some distance to go on many fronts, we must understand that it was because the Framers stated and affirmed these principles that we were able to work toward establishing liberty and justice for all. Had the principles stated above not been embedded at the very core of our political founding, it is uncertain whether we could have undone the national disgrace called slavery or other deviations from the foundational truths.

"Conservative" indicates a desire to conserve the old ways. In some countries the old ways are things like monarchy or aristocracy, the preservation of stodgy traditions, and so forth. In the United States of America, being "conservative" means something vibrant and freeing. It means a commitment to the dignifying ideals of the American founding, especially:

1. Liberty and justice for all
2. Universal God-given rights
3. Equality of everyone before the law, meaning both equal protection and equal accountability
4. Free speech
5. Genuine (non-paternalistic) concern for neighbors
6. A spirit of curiosity and corresponding embrace of scientific inquiry and rigor
7. A general recognition that right and wrong exist

The ideals of the American founding stand starkly against racism, injustice, and slavery. It was *because of* the principles laid out in the Declaration of Independence that the scourge of chattel slavery was outlawed. In my lifetime I have never heard any conservative say they wanted to get back to racism or slavery, and such is not what "great again" means to any conservative I know. We take joy in everyone's freedom and flourishing. Rather, they seek a general recognition of the good ideals that allowed Americans to grow and flourish as one people from many backgrounds and become the most prosperous and decent nation on the face of the earth.

Each of the following chapters is essentially a short essay. Some (such as Chapter 11) have already become the subject of books by others.

I do not intend anything in this book to be quarrelsome. I prefer to be on good terms with every person. However, peace at the cost of truth harms many. I write plainly because present circumstances demand it. Let those who read understand that I am a friend to those who love truth and yearn for justice. I invite everyone to become such a person.

DB, Lovettsville, January 2023

---

1. As a Christian and a rational human I know that people are not basically good; every last one of us are sinful. We have a conscience that distinguishes right from wrong, but we also have a tendency to go against that conscience. That is, we are inclined to evil but regulated by conscience in varying degrees. When I use the term "good people," then, I do not suggest that anyone is fundamentally good. Rather, I mean "people who make some effort to recognize and do what is right."

2. Daniel Alan Brubaker, *By The People?: The 2020 U.S. Presidential Election And Theft of Americans' Right to Self Rule* (Lovettsville: Think and Tell, 2022).

3. Tulsi Gabbard (@TulsiGabbard), October 11, 2022.

INTRODUCTION

The culture of nations vary. A nation of any great size is home to multiple subcultures. The United States, though still young, are already a rich tapestry of people with many different backgrounds and stories. Our national motto, E Pluribus Unum "Out of many, one," certainly references the disparate states that joined together to form a federal government. However, the motto is also descriptive of a defining trait at the root of what might be called American culture: We are a people who value, and see ourselves as, unified (for example, around certain core principles) even while we recognize our various important differences.

America the Beautiful

Americans, in spite of our great diversity of thought, aspiration, and heritage, have been known abroad as self-assured, outspoken, sometimes even brash. We are risk-takers, creators, optimists, and doers. Typically, we are (or have been) confident in our identity and heritage as Americans. At the same time, we stand out in much of the world for a certain moral sensitivity rooted in a strong conviction that truth exists, that its pursuit is good, and that justice rests upon something more than mere societal consensus. This moral undercurrent is not confined to Americans of any ethnic group or national origin; it crosses all superficial boundaries.

The United States are among the most church-going societies in the world, and more Americans unapologetically believe in God than the people of most other nations. Our culture is neither original to this land, nor is it descended singularly from that of any other. This is to say, in culture as in ethnic heritage, we are a hybrid people. The term "hybrid" alone, however, fails to capture the essence of Americanism. Blending every culture in the world and treating every idea and proposition as though it were equally valid and deserving of elevation would yield nothing even vaguely resembling Americanism. Nor would it amount to anything even vaguely resembling "goodness." One distinctive feature of American culture, influenced undoubtedly by our substantial biblical and Judaeo-Christian heritage, is our widespread belief that certain ideas are true and/or morally good, while others are objectively false and/or morally wrong.

Americans' general belief that truth exists and can be found has led to the creation of an environment conducive to its open pursuit. This environment has been characterized, for example, by our fierce protection of freedom of speech and conscience, freedom of the press, the presumption of innocence, the equality of all people before God, and a consequent striving for equality of all people before the laws of the land. It also underpins the spirit of invention and scientific inquiry that has given rise to so many technological innovations that have in turn benefited humanity. These include electricity, the light bulb, the telephone, powered flight, computers, the internet, and various medical advances and discoveries.

The United States are a nation, in other words, whose foundation is a set of common affirmations and a promise. Our identity is not ethnic, because we do not have a single ethnic origin. What we hold in common is a commitment to the principles enumerated in the Declaration of Independence and applied to government in the United States Constitution, which established a system of rule by the people that includes many checks and balances to protect against tyranny. The sovereign in the United States is the people.

Are American[1] principles exceptional? Absolutely. However, they are not so because they are somehow particularly or uniquely American, but rather because they are true and good. The United States are (or have been) good because we affirm, in word with aspiration to deed, propositions that align with objective truth and justice. Many nations in history, ancient and modern, have attempted to claim that God was on their side, but they got it backward. The United States were founded in a humble but hopeful intention to be on God's side.

American principles have always been upheld by those who have taken up a position at the very center of basic Americanism, that is, a position in alignment with the U.S. Declaration of Independence, Constitution and Bill of Rights. These were aspirational documents that did not immediately reflect the reality of the situation among the states at the time they were adopted. Rather, they charted a course forward, navigating by certain fixed points among which was the proposition that all people are created equal, and so forth.

All unalienable rights are *negative,* that is, they indicate the limits of what government can do and never what government must provide. It was through direct appeal to the fixed points declared in these documents that the United States, a sovereign and self-governing nation, abolished their own pre-existing condition of slavery 89 years, 5 months and 2 days from the ratification of the Declaration of Independence, by means of a costly civil war (and over the obstinate objections of Democrats), and it was through appeal to these fixed points that she has made many other course corrections along the way.

Two Main Arguments

This book is divided into two sections, and also makes two related arguments. The first section and argument, comprising fifteen short chapters, is a sharp critique of the Democratic Party. The second section is a general discussion that includes a focus upon the semantics of the colors red and blue, including my assertion that the Republicans are properly the blue party and the Democrats are the red.

Until the mid-1980s, political maps in the United States were generally drawn with the Democrat states colored red, and the Republican ones blue. Then, in the late 1980s, U.S. media elites switched the colors on maps to red Republican and blue Democrat. I am convinced that this change was a calculated manipulation, a sleight-of-hand move made for reasons that I will discuss at greater length in Chapter 18. Over time, this change took root, and terms like "red state" became synonymous with Republican-majority states, and "blue state" with those under the control of Democrats. But Democrats today are as red as ever, and Republicans are not. I argue that it is time to change back the colors.

What does the term "Democrat" imply?

Words are not the things to which they pertain. They are symbols, and as such they can signify different things to different people and in different contexts. This is true of colors as mentioned just above, and also of labels such as Republican or Democrat.

When a person identifies with a political party, however, it is reasonable to conclude that they at least generally agree with the party's basic principles. So, when I learn that someone is a Democrat, I assume that they:

- support racism
- have a stunted or warped sense of justice
- affirm or excuse many kinds of immorality
- place politics above the safety and well-being of children
- are prone to magical thinking instead of rational and scientific engagement with the world
- are prone to resentment, rather than joy, at the success of others
- believe that the end justifies the means
- feel that they have a right to control others' lives
- are careless with data
- are economically illiterate

I sometimes learn over time that the *particular* Democrat lacks some of these traits. Maybe they do seem to care about children. Or perhaps they seem to believe in justice. Of course, if they lack too many of the traits, I am left wondering, *Why is this person a Democrat, since they diverge from the party on so many of its core priorities and objectives?*

The partisan divide in the United States is not entirely about misunderstanding. Increasingly, Americans have become committed to divergent beliefs about what is right and what is wrong, what constitutes justice, the definition of love, what it means to be kind, what is good and praiseworthy, and an array of other important topics. So, as I present my case, you may wish to consider whether you agree with what I assert to be good and true and fair.

Perverse Incentives: Power and Money

In considering who really drives certain societal problems, it may be helpful to notice who *benefits* from these problems existing in the first place. Which major U.S. political party:

- benefits politically and financially from racism?
- benefits from moral decline and social chaos?
- benefits from dividing people into identity groups, angry at each other and focused on difference rather than common dreams and goals?
- benefits from a massive and growing number of poor people who feel as though they have no opportunity for the future?
- benefits from the destruction that a culture of sexual promiscuity brings to young people's lives and futures?

- would be in trouble if people left welfare programs to become successful, stable and self-sufficient?
- benefits when people covet their neighbors' property?
- benefits from mass shootings?
- benefits if kids are dumbed down and set on a path to a destructive lifestyle and poverty?

We will discuss many of these topics further in the coming chapters, but if you answered "the Democratic Party" to all of the above, I believe you are correct. Now consider another list. Which political party benefits when:

- people start to see themselves as Americans and as brothers and sisters?
- racism and its expressions in American society actually recede?
- justice is done and everyone is treated fairly?
- kids of all backgrounds, sexes, and circumstances do well in school, get a good grasp of history and develop strong critical thinking skills?
- violent crime and property crime go down?
- people love their neighbors and take joy in the success of others?
- only those truly at the end of their rope access government safety net programs, and then only for as short a time as absolutely necessary?
- Americans preserve a strong sense of right and wrong, aspire to do what is right, and commend others who do the same?

If you answered "the Republican Party" to all of the above, again, I believe you are correct. In fact, if many of these things occurred, it would have a devastating effect on the Democratic Party's power and financial base. And, Democrat leadership and strategists know it.

Thinking about these questions may help you understand why things are really not as they seem. Incentives drive results. The fact that the Democratic Party would be in serious trouble without the existence and growth of racism and injustice gives them an incentive to try to preserve or even perpetuate those things. Of course, they try to do so without looking like that's what they are doing. But astute people understand that is what is going on.

On Group Identity

The United States were founded upon the affirmation of the individual, every individual, rooted in the proposition that certain rights, because given by God, belong to all people. Your rights, the American founders declared, belong to you because you are a human being created by God and in His image.[2] Virtually everything good that has happened in the history of our country has flowed in some way from this proposition. The proposition, it should be observed, is *deeply humanizing* and *intensely unifying,* because it recognizes and upholds the inherent worth and agency of every single individual. The proposition of individual rights also militates against the idea of group identity as the determining factor in anyone's fate. Yes, you may face challenges and some of those challenges will come in the form of ignorance or injustice at the hands of others. But you belong here, and no matter who you are, in this life you can overcome what comes your way.

Political party affiliation is a form of group identity. Is political tribalism therefore inherently un-American? Absolutely not. We choose all sorts of things with which to associate ourselves: Civic groups, churches or synagogues or mosques, charities, sports teams or clubs, organizations driven by causes, professional or learned societies, and yes, political parties. The point is that all of these are voluntary affiliations; you are not forced into any of them merely because of traits with which you were born. So, this is the important distinction. Your identity and future are not determined by your sex or your race or your physical traits. You can choose which way to go.

Roadmap

Chapters One through Fifteen deal with different manifestations of a sickness. Just as one sickness may have many different symptoms, or one symptom may be the cumulative result of several underlying conditions, so there is overlap between different Democrat policies and their root causes. For example, I cite Democrats' love-affair with Planned Parenthood as evidence of their racial bigotry, but also of their violence, immorality, tendency to infantilize, and abusiveness toward women and children. So, Planned Parenthood must be mentioned in multiple chapters.

In the final chapters, I discuss the colors red and blue, and then I pull back for some high level analysis before concluding with a summary of the grotesque carnage wrought by Communism everywhere it has been implemented over the past century and a half. Communist ideologues have had the United States in their sights for a century. They played a long game, and are now moving the pieces into place to subjugate us all to their slave system. The Democratic Party is the vehicle they intend to drive to their hoped-for glorious revolution.

A Note On Style

Throughout this book, unless quoting another source, I employ a convention of referencing races that are generally known by color designations not describe the true skin tone with quotation marks. Thus, "white" and "black." The description "brown" does not generally receive quotation marks, because it is the name of an actual color describing shade of skin.

I understand that there are other standards in our society today; my purpose, as with so much else, is to invite reflection. If any of us saw a person whose skin was truly either white or black, we might be shocked.

------

1. "American" principles did not appear out of thin air. They are rooted in an intellectual heritage in which England and the Netherlands figure prominently, and they are morally founded in the Bible. So, they are "American" only in (we might say) a secondary sense. They are the heritage of humanity, a fruit of a tree that providentially grew in the soil of liberty on this continent, eventually overpowering the weeds and brambles of slavery and many other injustices, but the tree could grow anywhere such soil exists.

2. Although the Declaration of Independence did not explicitly note the image of God, the proposition is implicit in the affirmation, because Genesis 1:27 is clearly the basis of the larger claim. Genesis 1:27 affirms the following: 1) "Man" in this context means men and women, 2) "created in the image of God" applies equally to men and women, 3) since all people, tribes, and nations are descended from Adam and Eve, all people therefore bear God's image.

YOUR LIFE MATTERS

Y ou belong here. You are not a blight on this world. Your breathing and consumption and emissions and building and inventing and traveling are all *natural*. Homes are natural. Cars, RVs, and airplanes are natural. Skyscrapers are natural. The internal combustion engine is natural. Nuclear and hydroelectric and coal and natural gas power are natural. We are human beings and all the products of our activity are, like those of animals with whom we share the planet, natural.[1]

You belong here, but you are not an animal. You share biology with animals: respiration with its astoundingly calibrated lacework of metabolic pathways, and so forth. But *you* are not your biology. You are something more, a soul. And, you know in your heart that there is a moral law governing the universe.

In this small book, I make moral statements. Notice that virtually everyone, even materialists who state that there is no God, make statements about right and wrong. We don't need to go deep into this matter here, but please consider that there is a basis for right and wrong that lies beyond mere human consensus.

You may agree with what I believe to be right or wrong at points and disagree at others. Where we disagree, both of us could be wrong, or one of us could be right. What we should know for sure is that it is simply not possible for two clear contradictory statements to both be true.

As we navigate through life, however, we should periodically remind each other that first, we all are here for a purpose, and second, we all ought to at least try to find what is true and do what is right. That is the reason I write, and I hope that you find this book useful.

---

1. Giving credit where due, I must acknowledge my professor of environmental chemistry, Norman Rose, for presenting this observation in a class lecture at the University of Washington around 1992. It has stuck with me ever since.

PART I

AMERICAN DEMOCRATS
ARE:

1

RACIST

The Democrat Party is [...] the most enduring monument to racism in America.[1]

Democrats regularly claim to be against racism while saying—and doing—very racist things. Many Democrats do not seem to consider themselves racist. When in front of cameras, Democratic Party candidates and operatives shed crocodile tears over racism while pointing their fingers at others. Yet speaking loudly against something while at the same time engaging in it is the mark of a hypocrite.

Although I will allege malice and overt racism to most Democratic party insiders, I do not ascribe it to every rank and file Democrat. Making false allegations is wrong (Exodus 20:16, 23:1, Deuteronomy 5:20, etc.), and only God knows for sure what is in another's heart. We can only infer based upon others' words and actions, and my principal objective is to address the *policy*: What are Democrats doing, what are the

actual effects, and what can we then infer about those who
drive such policies?

What Is Racism?

Racism could be defined so as to encompass everyone who
ever lived. As humans, our brains make preliminary snap
judgments about others based upon cues from our visual and
other senses. We cannot help it. No one can. Furthermore,
pre-cognitive reactions are an important survival mechanism
with biological reasons and benefits that include erring on
the side of caution during the short period between percep-
tion and cognition. Our interactions with the world around
us may start with reflexes, but they do not end there. Humans
are rational beings, meaning we generally have the ability to
think with complexity and in abstract terms. We are not
simple robots executing automatic responses to a stream of
stimuli. We decide how to interact with our environment
based upon our moral and rational engagement with initial
data.

In order for a term like "racist" to mean something other
than merely "being human," we should exclude our split-
second automatic perceptions and reactions from its
definition.

Rather, racism is the post-reflex differential valuation,
negative treatment, or antagonism of people based upon
their membership in a racial or ethnic category instead of
their traits as individual human beings, or the belief that
members of certain of these racial or ethnic groups are inherently inferior to others. Racism can be conscious or unconscious, and it can have varying degrees of malice, including
no malice whatsoever. Racism need not be driven by malice

in order to be harmful. This said, not all instances of racism are equally harmful or blameworthy. An expression of sincere and friendly curiosity about a person's ethnic story and background can sometimes be considered racist, but it is different in degree and perhaps even in nature from racially motivated violence, differential pay, or denial of equal justice in a court of law.[2]

I make a personal policy of extending grace to others. I have experienced racism that was both hurtful and harmful to me, but I have not dwelt on it or stopped caring for the persons who did it. I realize that there are many people in the world who have experienced far worse than I, and it is up to each individual to navigate such territory for themself.

The Core Problem With Racism

When we object to racism, it is worth remembering why we do so. There is much that could be said about the matter. Although I recognize that readers may come from many backgrounds, I root my discussion in the Bible.

First, the one who displays racism has forgotten that people are individuals, each one unique, made in the image of God (Genesis 1:27). Racism, which substitutes this important fact with a cartoonish reduction of people to no more than their physical traits, simply does not align with reality.

Second, racism is a violation of moral laws such as God's commandment to "love your neighbor as yourself" (Leviticus 19:18), with "neighbor" including even your enemies (Matthew 5:44-45, Luke 10:25-37), to "judge your neighbor fairly" (Leviticus 19:15), and to "do to others as you would have them do to you" (Luke 6:31). These are all ultimately the same commandment, the moral weight of which obligates everyone whether we acknowledge it or not. We *owe* each other justice. Of course, all the moral laws derive from the greatest one, to love God. It is *because* people are made in God's image that we are to judge them fairly, not slander them, or steal from them, or kill them, treat them as we would have them treat us, love them, and so forth. We are supposed to do that because by so doing we show love to God who made them and whose image they bear.

The foregoing is the real reason that racism is wrong,[3] and there is really no way apart from it to make a fundamental objection to racism at all. If people are mere animals and there is no moral law above the rules we arbitrarily set in society, then there is no way to assert that a society which rejects racism is any better than one that affirms it. Without the existence of a moral law, those two merely reflect different choices, both equally valid. But any honest person will admit they know in their heart that justice, right, and wrong exist. This fact is referenced in the Bible: Paul observed that whenever people who have no loyalty to, or familiarity with, the Scriptures instinctively do the things of God's laws, they demonstrate that it reflects something that's not random, but written on their hearts by their Maker (Romans 2:14-15).

Ultimately, any human decision to treat people as less than individuals of equal value before God is morally wrong. This is the problem with racism.

Are the United States Racist?

The American left today regularly asserts that the United States are an inherently racist nation, but their accusation is a projection.

Not only are the United States' founding principles incompatible with racism, they were a conscious rejection of it. Yes, slavery and racism existed on these shores at the time of our nation's birth, they held sway over many of our institutions for a period of time afterward, and they were and are grave evils. Chattel slavery has victimized members of all races around the globe and throughout history. It was not unique to the settlers of the New World. Indeed, slavery was embraced and practiced by a large number of the prior peoples whom they encountered.[4] Acknowledging this fact does not justify the practice, but it adds perspective.

Instances of racism occur virtually anywhere people exist, but if these run counter to a nation's *stated ideals* and if their manifestation in national government acts can be rejected by appeal to those ideals, then one cannot reasonably call that nation racist. The Declaration of Independence set out the United States' ideals and objectives in this matter when it said: "We hold these truths to be self-evident, that all men [i.e., all people] are created equal, that they are endowed by their Creator with certain unalienable rights, that among these are Life, Liberty, and the pursuit of Happiness."

Government systems can set laws and policies concerning what people *do*, but they can not repair the human heart. The United States charted a course immediately which affirmed as self-evident—*and non-negotiable*—ideals inconsistent with racism and chattel slavery.

Systemic Racism Does Exist

The United States are not systemically racist. Racism does exist in all political parties and in all societies because racism is ultimately a human problem, located in the human heart, an effect of our shared sinful nature. But not all people are equally racist, and the expression of racism is certainly not built into most of the American institutions as the left has recently alleged.

Racism is, however, a defining trait of the Democratic Party. If the racism disappeared the party would be unrecognizable. A non-racist Democratic Party would (among other things): support strict enforcement of immigration law; call Americans "American" rather than hyphenating non"white" people; help people get off welfare, EBT, Section 8, Obamacare, and into dignifying self-sufficiency; defund Planned Parenthood and stop pushing abortion in "black" communities; repeal unjust minimum wage laws; support requirements for voter ID; reject "equity" and support opportunity for all; reject "gun free zones" and "gun control" laws, which leave innocent people defenseless; end "Diversity, Equity, and Inclusion" programs; call to end racial quotas in hiring and admissions; support school choice; stop objecting to "brown" faces in advertising; reject race essentialism; stop venerating FDR and the "Great Society"; stop using the phrase "of color"; stop pushing patronizing "Black History Month"; stop acting as though they are owed allegiance of new immigrants and non"white" Americans; stop disproportionately attacking non"white" people who don't lean left; stop treating "black" Americans as though they are inferior to, and less capable than, everyone else; and condemn Antifa and BLM, both of which treat non"white" people as disposable pawns in a push toward Marxism.

Even more than half a century after the last publication of the Green Book,[5]—too many Americans still support the Democratic Party. This is despite the party's persistence in acting as though people of "black" and brown skin are morally, professionally, and intellectually inferior, and less worthy of life, quality education, a good job, safe neighborhoods, and competing as equals; in fact, less worthy in nearly every way.

The racist policies of Democrats are almost as astonishing as is their own air of superiority on the topic. That any large group of citizens would continue to nurture an opinion that some races are inherently better than others, in a nation founded upon the proposition that all people are created equal, should concern everyone. Given the dreadful past and present of the party, though, we ought not be surprised.

Current Overview of Democrat Racism

Democrats today are more obsessed with race than ever. They continually divide people into categories based upon skin tone and other physical features, and they insist upon judging people on the color of their skin rather than the content of their character.

In 2023, American Democrats still treat "white" people as the American norm, and all others as deviation from that norm. Democrats generally refer to "white" Americans, no matter how recently immigrated, as "Americans," but to "black" Americans, no matter how many generations removed from Africa, as "African-Americans." Americans of Asian descent, no matter how many generations removed from the Asian subcontinent, they call "Asian-American." Americans of Japanese descent, no matter how many generations removed from Japan, the call "Japanese-American," and so forth. To make matters worse, they don't even grant some people the courtesy of distinction based upon a historically defined ethnicity, but rather apply the term "Latinx" to a swath of people from many different parts of the world whom Democrats apparently have unilaterally deemed similar enough to be lumped together.

Democrats in 2023 still tend, especially, to treat "black" people as though they need saving, have no agency, have impaired or limited general competence, are not as intelligent as everyone else, don't know how to fill out forms or get and carry an ID to vote, are not good enough to compete for jobs or promotions or admissions without extra help or lowered standards, and cannot make a moral decision to do what is right rather than what is wrong. It is all so insulting.

Democrats in 2023 still support Planned Parenthood, whose founding purpose and enduring effect and (I believe) true aim to this day, is to diminish the number of "black" people in the United States.

Democrats in 2023 still demand different laws and rules based upon race, ethnicity, or national origin. At the U.S. border, their cynical attitude and expectation that "some" people are incapable of following the same laws as everyone else lures individuals—including children—into situations of grave risk for rape, assault, robbery, and even death from these factors during a crossing. Ongoing and increasing Democrat support for the non-prosecution and non-deportation of illegal immigrants rests upon a not-so-subtle insinuation that "some people" are morally or intellectually inferior and, perhaps even genetically, incapable of following the same laws as everyone else. Such a stance is a recycled version of the common racist argument that many Democrats made in the 1800s when they claimed that it was too dangerous to give slaves freedom or citizenship because their very genes made them morally inferior. Failing to apply laws equally to everyone, and failing to recognize that all grown people are capable of taking moral responsibility for their choices, however, is racist.

Democrats in 2023 still fight to keep many non"white" people from having a choice of schools for their children. They seem to prefer lining their own pockets, preserving their own political power through an unholy alliance with corrupt teachers unions, to the wellbeing of non"white" children. Never mind that the very future of those children may hinge upon the opportunities and guidance they are given during these precious formative years. If a "black or brown" child is kept in a vicious multi-generational cycle of dependence and despair, it is better for Democrats. That's why they will never allow any significant number of such kids an opportunity to escape.

Democrats in 2023 still support the existence and increase of a minimum wage. We will discuss minimum wage more later, but its most diabolical effect is to exclude many people from ever having the opportunity to step on the first rung of the ladder toward the American Dream. The minimum wage works hand-in-hand with the welfare plantation to keep millions of Americans, including a disproportionate number of "black" Americans, in a multi-generational cycle of dependence. This situation is great for Democrats, and is surely the reason that they are behind both policies.

The fact that all of the following people were Democrats gives a sense of the party's history on matters of race:

- **John C. Calhoun** (U.S. vice president 1825-1832, strong defender of slavery)
- **Andrew Jackson** (U.S. president 1829-1837, defended slavery and bought many more slaves throughout his life)

- **James K. Polk** (U.S. president 1845-1849, kept and purchased slaves throughout his life, defended slavery)
- **James Buchanan** (U.S. president 1857-1861, defended slavery and inappropriately influenced the U.S. Supreme Court in the Dred Scott case, today acknowledged to have been one of the worst Supreme Court decisions ever)
- **William Lowndes Yancey** (U.S. House of Representatives, later Confederate Senate, outspoken defender of slavery)
- **James Henry Hammond** (U.S. representative, U.S. senator, Governor of South Carolina, slave owner and open defender of slavery)
- **Jefferson Davis**, president of the Confederate States (former Democrat U.S. representative and Democrat U.S. senator)
- **Woodrow Wilson** (U.S. president 1913-1921, segregationist and defender of slavery; screened pro-KKK film *The Birth of a Nation* at the White House, Fabian socialist and founder of modern liberalism); lamented "the intolerable burden of governments sustained by the votes of negroes," and called the Klan "an 'Invisible Empire of the South,' bound together in loose organization to protect the southern country from some of the ugliest hazards of a time of revolution."[6]
- **Franklin Delano Roosevelt** (U.S. president 1933-1945, confined Americans of Japanese descent to internment camps, and major proponent of involuntary servitude in the 20th century)

- **Orval Fabus** (Arkansas governor 1955-1967, ordered the Arkansas National Guard to stop "black" students from attending Little Rock Central High School)
- **George C. Wallace** (Alabama governor 1963-1967, stood in the door to block Vivian Malone and James Hood from enrolling at the University of Alabama)
- **Lester Maddox** (Georgia governor 1967-1971, segregationist chosen as governor by Democrats in 1967, two years after he refused to serve "black" customers in his restaurant and then closed it altogether to avoid integrating; as governor denied Dr. Martin Luther King, Jr. the honor of lying in state after his assassination; endorsed George Wallace for president in 1968)
- **Theophilus Eugene "Bull" Connor** (Birmingham Commissioner of Public Safety 1937-1952, 1957-1963; Alabama Public Service Commission 1965-1972, white supremacist, enforcer of segregation, used fire hoses and police attack dogs against civil rights activists)
- **Harry Flood Byrd Sr.** (Virginia Democrat, major defender of segregation)

Have Democrats changed, or "flipped?" Hardly. Pick virtually any elected Democrat who supports Planned Parenthood, gun control, minimum wage laws or minimum wage increases, open borders, race-based reparations, DEI, or who opposes school choice, and so forth, and you will see mere adaptation of the core beliefs of a Bull Connor or a Woodrow Wilson to the modern political climate: insulting, demeaning, confining, disadvantaging, even killing non"white" people.

The Big Business of Racism

The prospect of racism diminishing in the United States terrifies Democrats. And why wouldn't it? To understand how the Democratic Party acts with respect to racism, and why at all costs it must never allow racism to decrease in the United States, we need only notice who benefits from racial grievance in this country, and what sort of situation the Democrats would be in politically if racial divides were healed. Racial grievance and division is the Democratic Party's bread-and-butter. They grandstand on it. They raise money off it. They build voting blocks upon it. They fan hatred with it. And, they use it to preserve and expand opportunity for their own election cheating operations. Do Democrats really want to see the realization of Dr. King's dream of a society in which everyone is judged by the content of their character and not by the color of their skin? Absolutely not.

If racial harmony were to erupt or increase, with Americans generally judging one another by the content of their character rather than the color of their skin or other factors unrelated to their innate worth as individual human beings (as indeed was the trajectory across the nation in the latter part of the twentieth century), Democrats would lose their major campaign issue! Who would benefit? Republicans, of course. Democratic leadership knows this, and therefore cannot allow racial division to ever diminish or disappear. The lion's share of Democrat political capital is the image of standing up against racists and "doing something" to solve inequities and to address the problems stemming from deep racial divides that have long plagued our country and that are supposedly fundamental and incurable.

The existence and spread of racism do three main things for Democrats. First, when "black" people (in particular) are harmed by Democrat policies, Americans (including most "black" people) blame Republicans. This is a political benefit to Democrats, and the greater the harm, the greater the benefit. With the help of a compliant media and academic establishment, it validates their preferred and carefully cultivated narrative about the United States, conveniently pinning blame on conservatives and Republicans in order to give the Democratic Party a soapbox issue. Racism is a problem. But it would be incorrect to imagine that it is driven by, or benefits, conservatives.

Second, the existence and spread of racism in the United States gives Democrats cover, and in many cases justification, for their own deeply racist attitudes, actions, and history. One of the worst things that could happen to the Democratic Party would be a situation in which most Americans of every background spoke of each other as "American," a single people united around principles of liberty and justice for all. This is what Republicans want. It would be a disaster for Democrats, and it is why Democrats' insist upon dividing people via "intersectionality," anger, offense, "triggers," and grievance groups. These things are bad for the soul and bad for society, but they are fantastic for Democratic politicians.

Third, I perceive that hurting "black" people quite simply satisfies Democrats' true conscious or unconscious racist disdain for them. Racism keeps a boot on the neck of "black" Americans especially, whom Democrats historically diminished and demeaned, holding them hostage to service of the leftist agenda while—so long as Democrats and their allies keep control of the narrative (which this book seeks to disrupt)—blaming their political opponents, the Republicans. So, the expansion of actual racist harm is a triple victory for Democrats, with most of the cost being borne by Republicans and "black" Americans.

Once you notice who benefits, Democrat priorities and actions begin to make perfect sense. Democrats will always *pretend* to address the problems of race but they do not really want to solve the issue for two big reasons: 1) They really are deeply racist, and 2) If the problem of racism ever gets solved, Democrats are in big trouble because they will be left without their premier issue.

So, here's what Democrats do: They pretend to be trying to solve the problem, as the ones who "get it," who really care, unlike the evil Republicans. They make a big show. Meanwhile, their every policy action is designed to keep certain racial groups down and dependent. A Democrat often supports programs for a Democrat-voting racial interest group, but she will always malign or actively oppose a good policy idea if it has the real effect of *helping* more members of that group than it hurts in the long run. Those things, such as school choice, welfare-to-work, jobs training programs that reduce the welfare rolls, right to carry in inner cities, abstinence education or anything designed to encourage marriage and faithfulness, make Democrats furious.

Democrat Racism Issues: Present

Following are some examples of ways the racism of the American Democratic Party manifests today.

Diminishing some Americans by hyphenation or ethnic designation as a regular matter of reference. What does it take to just be called "American?" For Republicans, you are American—plain and simple and with no extra qualifiers needed—if you hold American citizenship. For Democrats, however, it seems to be a little more complicated.

"Of color." This term, advanced and favored by American Democrats, is a demeaning racial designation that separates the world into only two broad classes of people. Its use seems to stem from Democrats' white supremacist sentiments, in that it lumps all of humanity under this label, "of color," giving only one race, "white" its own distinct designation.

Segregation and Division. Democrats have long made a policy of barring "black" Americans from full participation in the blessings of America by way of what they previously termed "separate but equal." In the mid-20th century, this policy took the form of segregation, assignment of separate facilities from schools to drinking fountains, to sections of restaurants and public transportation, and so forth. The message from Democrats to non"white" Americans rang loud and clear: "You are unclean and unworthy, so stay away from us." Ultimately, just as they do with hyphenation, Democrats persist in excluding "black" Americans from full inclusion in American society, though now more subtly. Apparently for this same reason, and also to foment division and advance a view of the United States as fundamentally flawed, Democrats proposed a song to be a separate National Anthem for "black" people ("Lift Every Voice and Sing" by James Weldon Johnson) that makes no mention of America (merely vague reference to "our native land") but that by inference essentializes America's past as uniformly "dark" and "gloomy." In fact, the "Lift Every Voice and Sing" says *nothing* positive about the United States' founding, ideals, good qualities, or aspirations. It makes no praise of the United States whatsoever.[7]

Socialism and the Welfare Plantation. Why was it Democrats who embraced socialism soon after the abolition of slavery, and not Republicans? It was no accident, and I believe it is the biggest single piece of evidence that the philosophical core of the Democrat Party has never changed. I will deal with the involuntary servitude aspect of socialism (that is, the general fondness of forcing some people into involuntary servitude to others, without particular reference to the racial dimension) in Chapter 10. However, the racist aspect of socialism is clearly part of the picture. When FDR pushed his socialist "Great Society," it was in the wake of the South's defeat in the Civil War and the various subsequent efforts by Democrats to continue subjugating "black" Americans in the context of the new reality which now included the 13th and 14th Amendments. Jim Crow laws were overt. The Great Society was a more subtle initiative to keep people already near the bottom—a space which at that time contained a disproportionate number of "black" Americans—from ever climbing out.

The hard bigotry of low expectations. During and after the fight for abolition, one of the major arguments that Democrats made against giving full rights and/or the vote to Americans of African descent was a claim that they were morally inferior, and that this inferiority was inherent genetically. Their argument was that those of African descent are not as capable of understanding and following laws as are the enlightened people of European heritage. It was false. Democrats' mistaken belief came from an inaccurate view of humanity. But Democrats have never rejected this argument; they are still making it! Democrats regularly suggest that immigrants are non"white" people, and that immigrants are incapable of understanding or following the same laws as everyone else.

Support for racism in hiring. Affirmative action, when based upon race or ethnicity, is a racist policy both on the face and in its outcomes. Affirmative action purports to help rectify a historic disadvantage of members of racial minority groups in employment or admissions. In recent years, affirmative action has increasingly been carried out under the label "Diversity, Equity, and Inclusion (DEI)." Whatever we call it, judging people by their race or other identity traits rather than their skills, qualifications, or content of their character is yet another example of virtue signaling that in this instance (like so many others) does clear and lasting harm to those it pretends to help. People of all races have generally similar innate potential and intelligence, yet when there is an artificial or externally imposed differential advantage given to any member of a group, it calls into question the competence of *any* member of that group. Did they get the job or admission because of outstanding effort and skill, or because they filled a quota despite being unqualified? It is an insulting shadow to cast over any human being. Furthermore, this approach cultivates division and resentment between members of different groups and demotivates people of all groups from striving for improvement. If you are in the category (for example, "white" or Asian) of those disadvantaged by DEI, the thought becomes "Why should I even try? I am not going to be rewarded for my efforts." If, in contrast, you belong to the category of those advantaged by DEI, the thought becomes "Why should I even try? I'll be rewarded regardless of my efforts." The remedy for historical wrongs is present fairness. All kinds of people should be challenged to improve themselves, to rise to the height of their individual potential in an environment of opportunity. It is the best and most dignifying policy.

The dirty secret of affirmative action or DEI today is that it truly keeps members of the "protected" classes down far more effectively than even the most malicious racist hiring managers (which today are probably few and far between) could dream of doing. The bonus for Democrats is that DEI locks members of the "protected" class into a second-tier category of citizenship—both in their own eyes and in those of others who are encouraged to see them as "needing" special lowered standards—while Democrats pretend to help. It is a victory for Democrats who in truth scorn non"white" people and seek to keep them away from self-sufficiency, independent achievement, and economic success. DEI perpetuates grievance and ensures that there will never be an even playing field. As an added benefit, Democrats can demagogue against anyone who even suggests doing away with it, calling *them* racist! Life really could hardly get sweeter for a Democrat.

Affirmative action ensures that achievement for any person it "helps" will never be fully recognized by others. Think how it would feel if you were a top achiever. Imagine *never* escaping others questioning the reason for your success. Some readers, sadly, know *exactly* how it feels, because they have lived as "beneficiaries" of affirmative action all their lives, and they hate it.

Gun control in general. "Gun control" may be discussed further in multiple chapters ahead. The data on gun restrictions is extensive and conclusive: Instituting "gun free" zones and restricting the freedom of regular citizens to carry a firearm lead to enormous increases in victimization crimes such as rape, theft, robbery, murder—and the accompanying economic devastation—where such policies are instituted. And who pushes policies that wipe out "black and brown people" but Democrats, with their two-pronged drive for gun control and Planned Parenthood? Top Democrats know how to read data just like anyone else. They know exactly what they are doing. But for Democrats, an increase in deaths of dark-skinned people is a victory because it gives them more to blame on Republicans, while also moving closer to their objective of centralized authoritarian government. So, Democrats always push especially hard for gun control in areas with more concentrated "black" populations. Then, when things get bad *as they always will when law abiding citizens are defenseless*, the same Democrats call for more of the policies that caused things to go downhill in the first place. The dreadful cycle continues endlessly. Gun control laws are among the most racist laws in America.

"Gun-free" schools. Particularly insidious is Democrats' preference for "gun-free" policies in schools, which serve not only to increase the general likelihood of a mass shooting incident as well as the prospect of a perpetrator inflicting large numbers of casualties before being stopped, but disproportionately serves to increase the likelihood of injury and death to "black" students, since such policies are especially implemented in parts of the nation with greater concentrations of such students.[8]

Democrat Racism Issues in Summary: Years Past

Historic manifestations of Democrat racism are many. Below is just a sampling to serve as vignettes.

Segregation. FDR and later Democrat presidents and congresses worked to keep public schools segregated. Democrat Woodrow Wilson famously re-segregated the U.S. military after it had been desegregated. In my own locality of Loudoun County, Virginia, Democrats fought to keep schools segregated for a very long time.[9]

Redlining. Redlining is a process of denying loans and other economic opportunities to residents of certain localities. It was Franklin D. Roosevelt (FDR) who first instituted a policy of redlining, which harmed non"white" people and kept neighborhoods racially segregated by (among other things) setting residents of minority communities or integrated communities at a financial disadvantage in terms of ability to borrow money. While it is not inappropriate for lenders to take actual risk into account when lending and setting interest rates, practices like redlining that make sweeping generalizations based upon factors with little or nothing to do with likelihood of repayment are unfair and discriminatory. And the disadvantages created compound over time. Redlining's successor policy, the Community Reinvestment Act (CRA), was also pushed by Democrats. Like redlining, the CRA resulted in disproportionate harm to "black" Americans since it forced lenders to make loans to those likely to default. This misguided Democrat policy led to the subprime lending crisis which ultimately displaced many Americans from homes and cost taxpayers billions of dollars in bailouts for the lenders whom the government forced into bad deals.

Internment of American citizens of Japanese descent. During World War II, Democrat FDR in 1944 issued Executive Order 9066, rounding up American citizens of Japanese descent, depriving them of their liberty based not upon any specific case-by-case evidence that particular individuals posed a threat to American national security, but based upon a racist presumption that any American of Japanese ethnicity is liable to support the Japanese, America's enemy in that war. In so doing, Roosevelt was acting unconstitutionally, but the Supreme Court affirmed his decision, and it was observed that eight of the nine justices at the time were appointed by him, and every one of the six justices who supported FDR's order were his appointees to the Court. The lone justice appointed by Republican President Herbert Hoover, FDR's predecessor, dissented, asserting that the internment was unconstitutional.

Slavery, the KKK, and Jim Crow. It is well-known that the Democrat Party defended the institution of slavery, that the KKK was formed by Democrats, that Jim Crow was the Democrat response to their loss of the Civil War.

Erection of Confederate monuments by Democrats in the late 1800s and early 1900s to dominate public spaces with visible reminders of an oppressive past—and to administer a daily poke in the eye to those whom they had earlier held in bondage, and their descendants.

Blocking a "disobedient" "black" woman from appointment to the U.S. Supreme Court and attempting to block a "disobedient" "black" man. In 2003, George W. Bush nominated the highly qualified Judge Janice Rogers Brown to the U.S. Court of Appeals for the District of Columbia Circuit, and she was immediately recognized as a potential nominee to the U.S. Supreme Court. Rogers Brown was an American success story, the daughter and granddaughter of sharecroppers who grew up in Alabama. Her family had refused to enter restaurants with separate entrances for "black" customers. She put herself through college and law school (UCLA), and served seven years as an associate justice of the California Supreme Court, as the first "black" woman in that role. "But she was an outspoken conservative—so [Senator Joe] Biden set out to destroy her."[10] Biden successfully filibustered her appointment to the D.C. court, but she made it through on a second nomination and by 2005 was on Bush's short list of potential nominees to the Supreme Court. She would have been the first "black" woman ever nominated. Biden went on CBS's Face the Nation and threatened a filibuster if she were nominated to the Supreme Court: "I can assure you that would be a very, very, very difficult fight and she probably would be filibustered." Writes Marc Thiessen, "What Biden threatened was unprecedented. There has never been a successful filibuster of a nominee for associate justice in the history of the republic. Biden wanted to make a black woman the first in history to have her nomination killed by a filibuster." In the end, Bush nominated Samuel Alito, Jr. instead of Rogers Brown.

Democrats enforce their orthodoxy, but they reserve an extra measure of fury and vitriol for "black" people who "stray" from the Democrat plantation.

Patronizing

"Virtue signaling" is the cynical practice of doing something that looks virtuous to others but has no positive effect in solving a problem. It often makes things worse. People who virtue signal do not really care about making the world better; they only care what others think of them.

In a 2005 interview with Mike Wallace for 60 Minutes, Morgan Freeman took Wallace—who was advocating the traditional Democrat position—off his guard:

WALLACE: Black History Month, you find...

FREEMAN: Ridiculous.

WALLACE: Why?

FREEMAN: You're going to relegate my history to a month?

WALLACE: Oh, come on.

FREEMAN: What do you do with yours?

WALLACE: [silence]

FREEMAN: Which month is White History Month?

WALLACE: [searching for an answer]

FREEMAN: Come on...tell me.

WALLACE: Well...[confident change of tone]...I'm Jewish.

FREEMAN: [apparently annoyed by the evasion] OK. Which month is Jewish History Month?

WALLACE: There isn't one.

FREEMAN: Oh...oh. [pause] Why not? Do you want one?

WALLACE: No, no.

FREEMAN: I don't either. [pause] I don't want a Black History Month. [pause] Black history is American history.

WALLACE: How are we going to get rid of racism until...?

FREEMAN: Stop talking about it. [pause] I'm going to stop calling you a white man. [pause] And I'm going to ask you to stop calling me a black man.

Whatever Freeman's broader political sympathies, it is worth noting that he had a major role in perhaps the single most conservative film of its decade: *The Lego Movie*, in which the totalitarian villain (Lord Business, "the Micromanager," played by Will Farrell) tried to force all of society to conform to his wishes, failing to recognize that the world is most beautiful and productive when people are free to choose their own way, to create and do and build according to their own unique gifts and abilities. The film honors differences among people while also recognizing that there is right and wrong. I have long wondered at such a strong conservative message emanating from Hollywood.

Victimization of Non"White" People

The biggest modern assault on "black" and "brown" people might have been Democrats' expansion of welfare programs in the 1960s. Presented as a "compassionate" means of assistance, it was not. In the United States, welfare programs are diabolically crafted by Democrats to erect barriers and to remove opportunities from formerly disadvantaged groups at the very moment in history when the winds of change promising true opportunity were blowing in the wake of the dreadful effects of slavery. At this moment, the Democratic Party faced true danger and had to find new ways to keep as many members of this group as possible down. At the same time, they wanted—and increasingly needed—the actual political support of "black" people. They found a way to achieve both.[11]

Treating "Black" Conservatives Like Runaway Slaves

One example highlighting the unbroken link between Antebellum Democrats and Democrats of today is the cynical treatment of "black" people not as individuals with human dignity, but as disposables to be used and discarded in the pursuit of the masters' priorities and enrichment.

Frances Fox Piven and Richard Cloward have long been heroes of the American left. In 1966 they wrote,

> The national Democratic leadership, however, is alert to the importance of the urban Negro vote, especially in national contests where the loyalty of other urban groups is weakening. Indeed, many of the legislative reforms of the Great Society [that is, FDR's massive implemented of 'welfare' in

the 1930s] can be understood as effort, however feeble, to
reinforce the allegiance of growing ghetto constituencies to
the national Democratic Administration.[12]

In other words, "black" people (or as Cloward and Piven
call them, "the urban Negro") are pawns to be held in
bondage to Democrats by dependence upon Democrat-
supported welfare. Democrats and marxists have long treated
"black" people not as humans and fully equal citizens, but as
property whose value is measured by its usefulness. Accordingly, when a "black" person dares to leave the Democrat way
of viewing the world, and especially if they become successful, a fury is unleashed upon them unlike that experienced
by members of any other race. People like Clarence Thomas
(referenced above), Thomas Sowell, Herman Cain, Star
Parker, Larry Elder, Carol Swain, and Stacey Dash among
many others have all been at the receiving end of Democrat
hate. Candace Owens offered an explanation:

> White liberals hate black conservatives because we don't
> see ourselves as oppressed. Fundamentally, because we see
> ourselves as their equals. That's the issue.[13]

Against "Black" People

Although their racial animosity and patronizing condescension extends to every racial group, Democrats have always
reserved a special scorn for "black" people. Whereas
members of other races are often treated as competent and at
least excused when they achieve success without special
assistance, such is not the case for "black" people, particularly those who do not pay lip service to a leftist narrative.

Democrats' scorn for "black" people, and push to limit their increase and success in society, is today most evident in three major Democrat policy priorities which all especially cause victimization of "black" Americans: Gun control, opposition to school choice legislation, and abortion. All three policies do grave specific damage, but perhaps nowhere is Democrat scorn for "black" people more evident than in their almost fanatical support for elective abortion in general and abortion provider Planned Parenthood specifically. And, not coincidentally, Planned Parenthood to this day disproportionately focuses it clinics and abortion operations in areas with heavily "black" populations. According to Voddie Baucham,

> Black women make up around eleven percent of the population, but a third or more of the abortions. Black and Hispanic women combined, around a quarter of the population, more than half of the abortions. In major cities in the U.S., more than half of all pregnancies of black women end in abortion. We've been targeted since the onset, before Planned Parenthood, and Margaret Sanger's 'Negro Project.' We've been targeted by abortionists. And now, to see black people flock to a party whose platform and history has been dead-set on their annihilation boggles my mind.[14]

Against Asian People

Unfortunately, Franklin Delano Roosevelt's internment of Japanese Americans was not an isolated example of anti-Asian sentiment, policy, and action by Democrats. As I write, I sit in Loudoun County, Virginia, where woke Democrats have ganged up on schools to force students of Asian ethnicity to reach a far higher standard than others in order to gain admission to sought-after high school and university programs. At Virginia's Thomas Jefferson High School for Science and Technology in late 2022, it became known that National Merit Scholarship notifications were withheld from students, most of whom were of Asian descent, in pursuit of "equity." Not far from there, "equity" became an excuse for hindering admission of Asian heritage students to the elite Academies of Loudoun compared to students of other races. All these policies were driven by Democrats.

Against Jewish People

Antisemitism has long run deep among Democrats. The New York Times, a bastion of the left, famously hid the horrible reality of the Holocaust even after they confirmed what was going on.[15] Today, the Democratic Party picks sides with all kinds of enemies of the Jewish people, and antisemitic rhetoric, sentiment, and graffiti are sharply rising in the United States. Furthermore, Democrats have embraced leaders who advance antisemitic sentiment such as Minnesota Rep. Ilhan Omar and Michigan Rep. Rashida Tlaib.[16]

Where antisemitic hatred rears its head, therefore, it's a good bet that the government and population are heavily Democrat. In May of 2021, an ADL report showed a "sharp rise in anti-Semitism" in overwhelmingly (~97%) Democrat Washington, DC from 2019 to 2021. And, DC—which is a fraction of the size of the state of Virginia in both population and territory—had *virtually the same* number of antisemitic non-assault incidents as its neighboring state. To top it off, Virginia had zero antisemitic assaults either year, while DC

had two in 2020.[17] A review of the ADL data for all anti-
semitic assault incidents from 2019-2022 show most states
(including most big historically conservative ones: Alabama,
Alaska, Arkansas, Georgia, Idaho, Indiana, Iowa, Kansas,
Mississippi, Missouri, Montana, Nebraska, North Dakota,
Oklahoma, South Dakota, Tennessee, Utah, Virginia, West
Virginia, and Wyoming) with zero incidents. But the major
Democrat strongholds of Washington, DC (4 antisemitic
assaults), Massachusetts (7 assaults), New Jersey (22 assaults),
California (41 assaults), and New York (170 assaults) told a
different story.[18] Antisemitism is indeed a problem. And, it is
overwhelmingly not a problem of the typically Israel-friendly
right, but a sickness manifesting most among those who
identify as Democrats.

It is true that several of the states above with many antisemitic assaults also have large Jewish communities, and this
fact may play a role in the data—either in terms of reporting
or in terms of the likelihood of events. I've not done a study
controlling for variables and accounting for sources of error, I
am merely discussing results from the ADL reports that have
been in the news.

Democrats Consider Muslim A Race

There are some 2.5 billion people calling themselves Christians all over the world, in every ethnic group and country.
Christians are not a race; they are people bound together by a
common set of beliefs. Having a disagreement with the
historic Christian faith may be right or wrong, but it would
not be racist. Likewise, there are some 1.9 billion people
calling themselves Muslim all over the world, in every ethnic
group and country. There is great variety in Islam, which has

sects and subgroups. For one of the best summaries I have yet seen, I recommend my mentor Andrew Rippin's excellent book, *Muslims: Their Religious Beliefs and Practices.*

By law, prospective immigrants to the United States who are members of "the Communist Party *or any other totalitarian party*" are denied entrance to the country.[19] The definition "totalitarian party" applies to ISIS, al-Qaeda, and other radical Islamic groups that openly seek the destruction or subversion of the United States. "White" Americans, most famously Anwar al-Awlaki, and British nationals of various races have famously joined these groups. Only an ignorant person who has no sense of the ethnic diversity of the world's 1.9 billion Muslims would generalize "Muslim" as a race, or say that any disagreement with or criticism of some expressions of Islam is racist. Yet, Democrats often refer to policies, such as President Trump's 2017 temporary travel ban on entry from certain countries hosting such totalitarian groups and from which there was no reliable way to discern whether immigrants had joined them, as "racist." In so doing, these Democrats have—once again—identified themselves as the real racists for making the demeaning assumption that ideological identification with certain radical Islamic groups is racist.

How To Spot A "White" Supremacist

The only time I notice Democrats' reducing their commitment to white supremacy is when white supremacy is publicly spotlighted. Otherwise, Democrats are typically onboard.

How can you know if someone is a "white" supremacist? Here are some clues. They:

1. infantilize non"white" people
2. refer to non"white" people as "diverse"
3. support Planned Parenthood
4. support expansive long-term welfare programs, and erect barriers to escape which disproportionately harm non"white" people, especially "black" Americans
5. attack the character and intelligence of "black" Americans who disagree with them
6. fiercely oppose abstinence education in areas with heavy non"white" populations[20]
7. hyphenate non"white" Americans
8. oppose school choice in non"white" localities
9. tokenize and/or fetishize non"white" people
10. support "diversity, equity, and inclusion" programs
11. support gun control
12. favor open borders and excuse illegal immigrants
13. exhibit the bigotry of low expectations toward members of selected non"white" races
14. perpetuate ethnic or racial division
15. act as though non"white" people can't really embrace American culture as their own

Most Democrats—at least those in party leadership or elected office—meet the above criteria. Is anyone surprised that members of the party that founded the KKK would exhibit such traits?

As mentioned earlier, racist Democrats engineered a clever multi-pronged strategy for victory. First, with the help of a leftist media and leftist academic establishment, in the 1960s they presented as fact a nonsensical "flip" of the two parties. Once this myth got a foothold in the national psyche,

Democrats became free to continue perpetrating their own bigotry while being portrayed as the actual *opponents* of racism. For decades and even now, a major part of Democrat fundraising and victory strategy rests upon *not* solving the racism problem, engaging in racism actively, and actively and aggressively working to make it worse by picking at scabs to prevent healing while pretending to care.

Democrats need grievance to be bad so that voters will continue to be mad about it and keep voting for Democrat candidates who are *helping* you, are *fighting for you,* and are *on your side.*

Infantilization of Non"white" People

On February 25, 2022, Democrat Joe Biden nominated Ketanji Brown Jackson to the U.S. Supreme Court. His primary reason for doing so? She was a "black" woman. Now, there is no problem nominating any qualified person to the Supreme Court, but that is precisely the point: Joe Biden did not pick Jackson because of her qualifications, abilities or skills—not primarily, at least. Nor did he allow her to contend for the spot on full and equal footing with her fellow human beings. No, Democrat Joe Biden apparently did not think highly enough of "black" people to imagine that Jackson could possibly stand up as the best candidate unless extra, and indeed primary, weight was given to her race and sex.

We will have more to say about Democrat's tendency to infantilize those they look down upon in Chapter 12. For now, it is sufficient to mark the racial dimension of such.

Anti-immigrant

Because of the blessings of liberty to be found on our shores, many people wish to immigrate to the United States one day. Healthy immigration levels are important to the life of the nation by admitting good people who love the United States. A too-rapid pace and scale of immigration is harmful, over-whelming the system without sufficient time for assimilation.

Democrats' open opposition to enforcement of immigra-tion laws is cynical and racist, not to mention cruel and unjust. And Democrats have very little regard for immigrants, particularly those who are not "white." The most respectful policy for immigration is one that treats prospective immi-grants as human beings, equal before the law, deserving of fairness and capable of following the same rules as everyone else. Current Democrat policies treat those who follow the law by waiting their turn as though they are chumps.

Democrats, that is, want nothing to do with fairness at the border. The Biden administration is merely the latest to cheer his party's violation of the will of the people as expressed in immigration laws they passed through their representatives. He seems to perpetuate the old Democrat argument that "some people" are genetically incapable of following the same laws as "civilized" "white" people. The result is a breakdown of the fabric of American society as more and more people who do not respect rule of law flood into the country and transform us into a chaotic society.

Offended by brown faces

Democrats in recent years have made a show of cancelling dark-skinned mascots in places of honor in corporate America. Their attempts at virtue signaling were revealing. To Democrats, the dark-skinned Aunt Jemimah, Uncle Ben, Land-O-Lakes Native American woman, the Cleveland Indian and the Washington Redskin were evidently offensive, while the light-skinned Quaker Oats man, Mr. Clean, Sourdough Sam, Pat the Patriot, and Cap'n Crunch are just fine and may be retained as product and team mascots. As one internet meme quipped concerning the 2019 removal of the Land-O-Lakes woman, "Kick out the Native American, keep the land...sounds like standard Democrat operating procedure."

Protecting Racists In Their Ranks

One of the best ways to discern the relative attitudes toward racism in the two major U.S. political parties is to look at how they deal with the problem on those occasions when it occurs in their own ranks. And on this point, as on so many others, there is a stark difference between the Republicans and the Democrats.

Ralph Northam, while running for Virginia lieutenant governor in 2013, refused to shake the graciously extended hand of his Republican opponent, E.W. Jackson, who is "black", at the end of a televised debate. In early 2019, images of now Governor Northam's personal page from his 1984 medical school yearbook became a point of controversy. Of all possible photos that could have been chosen for this page, Northam appears to have picked one showing two people in costume, one wearing blackface and the other in a Klan hood. He later admitted that he was one of them, but did not admit which. However, Virginia Democrats were the party that had defended slavery and that was long the home of

Harry Flood Byrd, an ardent defender of segregation. Around that time, Northam said, "What I really want to do is talk about the racism and the hatred and bigotry that I have fought so long and hard for." His defenders stated that he had misspoken, but I believe it was a Freudian slip. Although former Vice President Joe Biden, as well as current Speaker of the House Nancy Pelosi, and the NAACP called for his resignation, Northam did not resign, and they did not press the issue. He completed his term, and Biden later gushed with praise for him.

Fear of being discovered

Most elected Democrats and their allies, of course, know enough of the history to understand who is really racist. For this reason, they must exercise gatekeeper controls in the media as much as possible. In 2022, Republican Winsome Sears was elected Assistant Governor of Virginia. As a "black" woman holding such office in a bastion of the Old South, her election was historic. However, Democrat activist journalists acted as though it had not happened, and for the most part refused to give her a platform. Commented Sears (referencing Northam), "I wish Joy Reid would invite me on her show...She talks about white supremacy. Does she know that I ran against a white supremacist?"[21]

Reparations

During the Civil War, an order by Union General Sherman proclaimed an allotment of land to some freed families, "40 acres and a mule." Certainly, it would have been right in many cases to require such a restitution from the actual enslavers to the actual enslaved. After Abraham Lincoln's assassination, however, his Democrat successor Andrew Johnson sought to modify the order. Many former slaves did acquire land in various ways, whether through homesteading or outright purchase, despite the fact that most of the lands they had worked as slaves were restored to the former owners. The details of what occurred at that time are complex, and it is obvious that—while abolition itself was an outworking of justice for those who had been enslaved— proximal justice was not full in terms of restitution paid to victims by those who had forced their labor over many years or decades.

Justice requires the punishment or restitution from the guilty, and the vindication or payment to the individual or individuals who were harmed. To throw a third party in jail or require them to pay restitution is not justice. Similarly, people who were not among those harmed do not typically have a claim, even against the actual perpetrator.

Calls for reparations today—yes, coming from Democrats, though not from all Democrats—turn past injustices into a vehicle for present racism. Representative Burgess Owens stated,

> At the core of the reparations movement is a distorted and demeaning view of both blacks and whites. It grants superiority to the white race, treating them as an oppressive people too powerful for black Americans to overcome. It brands blacks as hapless victims, devoid of the ability which every other culture possesses, to assimilate and to progress...proponents of reparations believe that black Americans are incapable of bearing their own burdens, while white Americans must bear the sins of those who

came before them. Proponents do not take into account the majority of white Americans who never owned slaves, who fought to end slavery, or who came to America long after it was ended. This divisive message marks the black race as forever broken, a people whose healing can only come through the guilt, pity, and benevolence of whites...those who seek reparations have accepted the theory that skin color alone is capable of making one race superior to the other, that with no additional effort, values, or personal initiative, white Americans will succeed, while black Americans will fail. At its very core, this represents the condescending evil of racism.[22]

It is difficult to imagine 160 years after the passage of the 13th Amendment how these past injuries can be further rectified in a fair way. The actual victims, as well as the perpetrators, are all long dead. Furthermore, even at the time it would not have been right to require all white people, or even the nation in general, to pay restitution. If restitution was owed, it would have been from the actual owners of slaves and possibly also from those who helped them perpetrate their crime against the victims. The main entity which aided in the perpetration of this crime was the American Democratic Party. Perhaps the DNC could today be compelled to pay reparations to those it harmed a century and a half ago. I do not think that it practical, but one thing is certain: It is not right to blame an entire race—such as white people in general—for slavery. And it is not right to blame anyone whose family immigrated to the United States after the end of slavery. Nor is it dignifying to treat all "black" people today victims of slavery. If anything, "black" people today are far more appropriately considered victims of current racist

Democrat policies and laws. If everyone stopped voting for Democrats, many of these injustices would dissipate.

In a nation where smart and hardworking businesspersons of any race regularly become multi-millionaires or even billionaires in a matter of years or decades, it seems far more productive and just today to focus upon ensuring that laws are applied equally so that everyone has the opportunity to succeed, than to focus on past injustices the actual parties to which are no longer with us.

Nonsensical Blame Shifting

The left's pattern of blaming Republicans for racist actions and outcomes for which they could not have been responsible sometimes reaches comical levels. But some people believe it. During the chaos of 2020, the city of Minneapolis came under fire during the Black Lives Matter and Defund the Police movements and riots. The subtext was that Republicans were to blame. Yet, it had been decades since Republicans had any significant sway in Minneapolis.

A college professor friend of mine, frustrated at the insulting insinuation that Republicans were to blame, wrote, "Minneapolis is a city with a Democratic mayor and a Democratic city council without a single Republican on it: Twelve of the 13 city-council members are Democrats, one is a member of the far-left Green Party. It has a progressive chief of police who was preceded by another progressive chief of police. Minneapolis sits in a state with a Democratic governor and a Democratic state house. Every statewide executive office in Minnesota is either held by a Democrat or is officially nonpartisan, including the office of Attorney General - currently held by former deputy chair of the

Democratic National Committee, Keith Ellison. Democratic Senator and former presidential candidate, Amy Klobuchar, was formerly the prosecutor for Hennepin County, where Minneapolis sits. She never brought charges in more than two dozen officer-involved fatalities that occurred during her tenure. There is not a single Republican as such holding a statewide office in Minnesota or a significant position in the city of Minneapolis."[23]

The "Southern Strategy" Myth

A common retort of Democrats who claim that the parties "flipped" is the citation of the so-called "Southern Strategy." There is not space here to fully develop a response to the allegations of a flip. I recommend that readers look to the work of Carol Swain on the topic. But consider, if the parties actually "flipped" then:

- why are the Democratic heroes from before the alleged "flip" (such as FDR and Woodrow Wilson, both of them racists and supporters of involuntary servitude, or John Dewey) not now heroes to the modern Republican Party and reviled by the new, enlightened Democrats?
- why are the institutions (such as the New York Times) that formerly aligned with the Democrats not now supportive of the modern Republican Party? Did the New York Times and other such institutions "flip" too? But, if they did, why then do they persist in glorifying the persons and policies of FDR, Wilson, and Dewey, for example, and those allied with them?

The answer, of course, is that the parties *did not flip*. The Democratic Party, sensing the winds of change, merely engaged in some fancy public relations maneuvering, repackaging its message of racism in a way that cleverly harnessed racial grievance toward ongoing Democratic political ends while also keeping it alive.

Confederate Flags and Monuments

In the decades following the victory of the anti-slavery Union in the Civil War, coalitions of Democrats pooled their resources to erect monuments to men who had fought so hard on behalf of the Confederacy. Across the South, bronze statues of Confederate officers and soldiers, and other such memorials, popped up in town squares, parks, and other public spaces. Without a single exception of which I am aware, Democrats initiated, funded, and oversaw the construction of these monuments, principally across the South. For a century, the monuments so placed served as painful reminders to the descendants of former slaves that powerful people in this society still dreamed of a past "golden era" when slavery was permitted.

How does one escape the consequences of their own actions? A common tactic is deflection. Bullies often accuse others of the things that they have done or are doing. As America progressed through the 20th Century and into the 21st, even some people who habitually voted for Democrats began to understand that slavery was rejected by most Americans. This fact posed a political problem for Democrats, as it meant their candidates would not continue to win unless they could find a way to reframe history, hiding or diminishing the ugly stain of their own long and continued support for slavery. In the early 2000s, therefore, Democrats began to make a big show of campaigning for their removal from public spaces.

I have found these campaigns to be humorous: If Democrats wish to remove their own monuments, why should I mind? But of course they seem to have hoped that Republicans would push back in order to bolster their fictional narrative that the parties somehow have flipped and that the Republicans are now the ones who would have defended slavery. It is clearly driven simultaneously by a broader Marxist push to destroy Americans' awareness of and sense of connection with the past, disorienting and dividing society in preparation for a communist revolution, as will be discussed in Chapter 11.

The only people in my own life whom I have ever known to display the Confederate flag have been Democrats. I do not recall ever seeing someone I knew to be Republican or conservative displaying the Confederate flag. This is not to say that the flag signifies sympathy for racism or the institution of chattel slavery to those who display it (I know that it is taken to mean these things to many others, and with good reason given the causes of the Civil War), and it is not to say that no Republican or conservative in the country today displays that flag, only that I don't recall seeing it.

Why Do Immigrants Often Vote Democrat?

While it is not true that *all* first-generation immigrant groups align strongly with the Democratic Party, it is very much the case for immigrants from some regions and countries. Given the strong racism of Democrats against people of brown skin, what can account for such a trend?

I believe the answer rests on multiple factors: 1) A positive view of democracy and an assumption (based upon the name and other factors) that the Democrats are the party that more fully represents democracy, 2) media misinformation and spin about Democrats and Republicans, 3) short-term self-interest, and, occasionally, 4) racism (mostly against "black" Americans) of some of the immigrants themselves. Let us consider each of these in turn.

First, people in much of the rest of the world aspire to live under democracy and its many benefits, and to these the United States still represents the democratic ideal. Most immigrants, as (indeed) most Americans, have a fairly un-nuanced understanding of the particular differences between pure democracy (which has never described the United States) and a democratic (or constitutional) republic (which is our form of government). Because the simple word "democracy" carries positive connotations worldwide, especially among those who seek to immigrate to the United States, it is natural that—especially among those very new or recent immigrants—the American political party whose name seems to embody the very democracy that led them to seek entry to America in the first place would be favored.

Second, the international media tend to be much more aligned with the perspective of the American left, and CNN is taken more seriously outside the United States than it is inside the country. Other media outlets either follow suit or march to the same drummer. When the world views U.S. events, it is often through the lens of CNN. Accordingly, people outside the United States usually see Democrats depicted as enlightened, forward-thinking, and caring, while Republicans are usually shown as backward, uncompassion-ate, and racist. For such reasons, immigrants often come to the United States with a pre-formed preference for the Democratic Party that is more rooted in the spin and bias of CNN and other left-wing media than in reality.

Third, immigrants are human beings and—like anyone else—are not immune to appeals to base self-interest. It is axiomatic that Democrats buy votes by promising and/or delivering "goodies" to those subgroups of people whose electoral favor they seek. By giving handouts to 50% or more of America (at the expense of the other 50%, of course), Democrats win over people who either do not understand that the carrot comes with strings attached, or whose concern is immediate and are willing to accept consequences for themselves or others "down the road." In many cases people simply do not consider the cause-effect situation: The current benefit is tangible and the consequence (if contemplated) is borne by someone else or merely theoretical.

Finally, some immigrants are racist, especially against "black" Americans. This is a strong factor, I believe, that explains why some segments of immigrants tend to strongly support Democrats. It is simply a matter of shared values...in this case shared values of negative opinions about "black" Americans.

Trolling "White" People

Democrats' support for books and movies with blatantly racist titles like *White Fragility*, *Why I'm No Longer Talking To White People About Race*, *Dear White People* and *Dear White Christian?* is yet another outworking of their need to perpetuate racial division. Take the first book, *White Fragility*, for example. The title is a catch-22, an overtly racist statement the mere recognition of which by any "white" person is intended to prove the book's thesis. Democrats in recent decades have begun to assert that it is not possible for a minority or oppressed population to be racist. That is utter nonsense. But remember, racism and racial division is the Democratic Party's bread and butter. Everyone has a sense of justice and we all know what racism looks and sounds like. Books or films insulting "white" people by essentializing or problematizing them solely based upon the color of their skin are certainly intended to be provocative and they serve the purpose of perpetuating racism and racial division, plain and simple. Exactly what Democrats need to do.

---

1. Mark Alexander, "The Democrat architects of white supremacy," Patriot Post, June 30, 2021. https://patriotpost.us/alexander/81007-the-democrat-architects-of-white-supremacy-2021-06-30.
2. Sometimes, certainly, true malice can be hidden under a facade of friendliness. However, this fact is certainly not reason to allege that all apparent friendliness is merely a facade. Often friendliness, even if ignorant or clumsy, is really just friendliness.
3. Someone may point out that the Bible reports God instructing the nation of Israel to keep itself separate from surrounding peoples, not to intermarry with them, and at times instructed them to put entire cities to the sword. However, God, at whose pleasure we live and in whose hands are all our days, also has the peculiar right to end our life at any time. The charge that God instructed his people to engage in what seems to meet our definition of racism (for example, by refusing inter-marriage), even if for only a period of time in their national history, does merit an answer. God's command stemmed from his care to keep his people separate from those he knew would harm them, in a precise historical context, and (most exegetes agree) for a limited period in the life of the nation, by causing them to follow after other gods. That it was about this fact and not race, one need only consider the Moabitess named Ruth, who was welcomed into the nation of Israel. Finally, when we discuss racism, we are talking about human judgment, not God's—and there is no sound biblical case to be made for anything resembling racism as a general operating principle for God's people today. Quite the opposite; see Galatians 3:28 or Ephesians 2:14.

4. "The Five Civilized Tribes were deeply committed to slavery, established their own racialized black codes, immediately reestablished slavery when they arrived in Indian territory, rebuilt their nations with slave labor, crushed slave rebellions, and enthusiastically sided with the Confederacy in the Civil War." Paul Chaat Smith as quoted in Ryan P. Smith, "How Native American Slaveholders Complicate the Trail of Tears Narrative," *Smithsonian*, March 6, 2018.

5. Taylor, Candacy, *Overground Railroad: The Green Book and the Roots of Black Travel in America,* New York: Abrams, 2020.

6. Tony Essex, "How Woodrow Wilson Tried to Reverse Black American Progress," *History*, July 14, 2020. https://www.history.com/news/woodrow-wilson-racial-segregation-jim-crow-ku-klux-klan

7. The idea of instituting the hymn as a "Black National Anthem" alongside the U.S. National Anthem came to wider attention during the BLM riots of 2020, with the National Football League (NFL) incorporating it in 2021. When Sheryl Lee Ralph performed the song at the 2023 Super Bowl adjacent to the National Anthem of the United States, Arizona Republican Kari Lake and others declined to stand for it. Lake's campaign team issued a statement telling the reason: "Our girl is against the idea of a 'black National Anthem' for the same reason she's against a 'white National Anthem.' She subscribes to the idea of 'one Nation, under God.'"

8. "U.S. Gunfire on school grounds occurs most often at schools with a high proportion of students of color—disproportionately affecting Black students." (What the cite fails to mention is that no schools which allow teachers to carry have such incidents, but Democrat politicians and administrators knowingly painted a target on the backs of these students by making their schools "gun free.") "Gunfire on School Grounds in the United States." *Everytown*. https://everytownresearch.org/maps/gunfire-on-school-grounds/. (5/25/22).

9. Matthew Exline, *We Have Been Waiting Too Long: The Struggle Against Racial Segregation in Loudoun County, Virginia*, 2nd ed. (Have History Will Travel Press, 2020).

10. Marc A. Thiessen, "Remembering the Black Woman Biden Blocked from the Supreme Court," *AEI*, February 1, 2022.

11. See also Star Parker, *Uncle Sam's Plantation*, Nashville: Thomas Nelson, 2010.

12. Piven, Frances Fox and Richard Cloward. "The Weight of the Poor: A Strategy to End Poverty." *The Nation*, May 2, 1966. https://www.thenation.com/article/archive/weight-poor-strategy-end-poverty/. (4/24/22).

13. Candace Owens, Twitter @RealCandaceO

14. Voddie Baucham, "Mark Dever on One Issue Voting," Stop and Think About It. YouTube, September 13, 2019. https://youtu.be/cuquvpUEsWE

15. Mark Levin, *Unfreedom of the Press*, (New York: Threshold Editions, 2019), 145ff.

16. Diane Weber Bederman, "Anti-Semitism has a history in the Democratic Party," *JNS*, March 20, 2019. https://www.jns.org/opinion/anti-semitism-has-a-history-in-the-democratic-party/

17. Eric Schucht, "Sharp rise in anti-Semitism in Maryland, Virginia and D.C., ADL reports," *Washington Jewish Week*, May 4, 2021.

18. "Audit of Antisemitic Incidents 2022," ADL Center on Extremism, March 3, 2023.

19. "USCIS Issues Policy Guidance Regarding Inadmissibility Based on Membership in a Totalitarian Party," U.S. Citizenship and Immigration Services, October 2, 2020. https://www.uscis.gov/news/alerts/uscis-issues-policy-guidance-regarding-inadmissibility-based-on-member ship-in-a-totalitarian-party; "Chapter 3 - Immigrant Membership in Totalitarian Party," U.S. Citizenship and Immigration Services.

20. Abstinence until marriage is one of the life-altering choices that greatly increases the probability of a person achieving later economic stability.

21. "Winsome Sears challenges Joy Reid to debate after 'dangerous' claim," *Fox News,* November 4, 2021.

22. Burgess Owens, "Why I Don't Want and Don't Deserve Reparations," Prager University, September 30, 2019. https://youtu.be/18tGOIvotFE.

23. Stan Watson, Facebook post, June 1, 2020.

2

HEARTLESS / ABUSERS

Near the beginning of the previous chapter, we defined the term "racism." We need to do the same here with the term "compassion." The word means "feeling with," and relates a sense of concern for the well-being of another person.

Being compassionate is not about pretending to care. Compassion relates to a true concern of the heart, and is proven to exist when one chooses that which is *actually* helpful to the other person over what *appears to others* to be helpful to the other person. When appearances are all that matter, compassion does not exist.

On nearly every major policy issue, you will find Democrats choosing to harm people, or to increase the likelihood of harm. In every example I will give in this chapter, the motive appears to be either the pursuit of *optics* favorable to Democrats or the pursuit of a *social or political agenda* to which Democrats assign higher priority than the actual safety and well-being of real people. Often both factors are involved simultaneously.

Democrats Invite Mass Shootings

Recently I delivered a spreadsheet from John Lott, listing shootings at U.S. schools over the past several decades, to my Loudoun County school board. I'd sorted it by whether law-abiding adults were permitted to carry guns on school grounds. Despite the fact that many states do allow this, I told them, one had to scroll through some 250 incidents (including all the well known mass-casualty tragedies) before reaching *a single shooting incident* at a school where adults could carry. And at these, there were only four entries. What were they? As I recall, one was a discharge outdoors with no injuries, another was an accident by a teacher while using the restroom before school hours (grazing her leg), and one was a suicide. None was a mass shooting.

That's right: All the major school mass-murder tragedies occurred at schools where law abiding adults other than resource officers or law enforcement personnel were *required to leave their guns in the car or at home.* And we know from the manifestos, actions, and journals of multiple mass shooters at schools and elsewhere, that they carefully avoid attempting their carnage in any place where there's a reasonable chance that ordinary citizens are armed. Furthermore, this fact about mass shootings is not only a matter of common sense, but it has been known from the data for decades.

Do Democrats know that simply allowing law-abiding adults to carry virtually ensures that there will never be a mass-shooting incident? Of course they do. This information is publicly available. But Democrats have a bigger agenda that, to them, is more important than the lives of children. Their hatred for guns overrides all else. They prefer people *feeling* safe to people *being* safe. It is heartless.

And, the matter is not limited to mass shootings; it is smaller scale victimization crime as well. When guns are outlawed, instances of rape, murder, mugging, and burglary increase. A stunning number of Democrats would rather a woman be raped or murdered before help arrives than allow her to carry a weapon that would have equalized the power dynamic and deterred or incapacitated the attacker. The reason is obvious: reducing crime was never their objective. Disarming society is the goal. This is why they love to talk about "gun crime," and you will rarely if ever hear them reference "crime" without a qualifier. That's because Democrats don't want to talk about "crime" overall. It would hurt their narrative.

Harming Kids Helps Democrats Politically

Like so many other categories of people, kids are useful but disposable pawns to Democrats. Indeed, similar to Democrats' stance on groups of people mentioned in Chapter 1, situations of murder or tragic harm to children quite simply give Democrats a political boost. Remember, Democrats need to have a problem they can pretend to solve. If they complain that guns are evil while there are no serious mass shootings, Democrats look stupid. They *need* the made-for-TV mass-casualty tragedies like an addict needs another hit.

As mentioned just above, Democrats can read data just like anyone else. They know that mass shootings only occur in places where citizens are not allowed to carry guns. This is why they push for more such places, whether schools or county buildings or libraries or DMVs.

Democrats' political need to harm children is not limited to the issue of guns. They harm kids in a multitude of other ways as well: indoctrination into marxist ideology, suicide "prevention" programs, "anti"-bullying programs, school closures and mask mandates during the COVID-19 pandemic, exposure to pornography and age-inappropriate explicit materials, learning loss and hindrance of higher-achieving kids in pursuit of "equity," forbidding abstinence education, indoctrination into "gender" ideology, and pushing surgical or chemical alteration of their bodies in the name of "gender" affirmation, to name a few. It is also possible that mandatory general COVID-19 vaccination of kids needlessly exposed millions of school children to health risks outweighing any possible benefits to this population group at near-zero danger of consequences from COVID in the first place.

Destroying Gender-Confused Lives Helps Democrats

Angry and damaged people are ideal voters for those who traffic in grievance. If the harmed people also require a life-time of medical services, that is money in the bank for the businesses that grow up around such clientele. If taxpayer dollars can be funneled to private businesses running the perpetual clean-up operation (often also Democrats and Democrat donors), the result is a self-perpetuating hustle that keeps all the harmed people *and* the crony businesses in the pockets of Democrats for the long haul. In other words, it is not about the long-term good of the people who were harmed. The hustle is all about creating more victims for political and financial benefit to Democrats. The poor people who got sucked in are, yet again, disposable pawns.

And their explanations don't even make sense! Democrats are a big ball of confusion and contradiction. They insist in one moment that male and female are arbitrary distinctions only in the mind and preference, but in the next breath they require surgical or chemical alteration of physical reality pertaining to male or female traits and features. Which is it? If being a man or woman has nothing to do with one's body, then why is altering the body necessary? Furthermore, what is the rational basis for asserting that there are dozens of genders? The answer, of course, is that there is none. The emperor, as they say, has no clothes. But Democrats (like the hucksters in Hans Christian Anderson's tale) present themselves as quite un-perturbed by such contradictions, and lash out with often vicious anger against anyone even asking these very reasonable questions.

The Welfare Trap

The dreadful effects of long-term dependence upon welfare programs were noted in the previous chapter. Although the welfare plantation does disproportionately affect people by race, the cruel harm of the system is not strictly limited to any particular race. All kinds of Americans are stuck in the multi-generational welfare trap, held there by soft barriers to escape. Here is how it works:

Various tragedies—often caused by Democrat policies such as Obamacare (which was designed, among other things, to drain the wealth of middle-income Americans), minimum wage (which erects barriers to entry that keep many prospective workers out of the marketplace, while simultaneously making it harder to run a profitable business), promiscuity and fatherlessness (pushed by Democrats as a way of destabilizing society and creating many more vulnerable people), the breakdown of order in inner cities (caused by bad policies, the prohibition of self defense via "gun control," and so forth), and others—push people into desperate situations in which they decide to fall back on a government "safety net." Programs such as Medicaid, Supplemental Security Income (SSI), Supplemental Nutritional Assistance Program (SNAP), Child's Health Insurance Program (CHIP), Woman Infant Child (WIC), and Section 8 housing assistance, among others, are examples.

However, Democrats have designed such benefits to be easy to obtain and difficult to leave. Many welfare recipients would have to take a reduction in pay and lifestyle in order to get off assistance and begin climbing the ladder. Plus, doing so takes effort. Many people, therefore, don't leave such programs. Democrats know it. So, masses of able-bodied and talented people lower their aspirations, deciding rather to stick with a reliable and non-judgmental government income rather than take the risks and difficulties of making their way in a competitive marketplace. So, this "compassion" is really an unhealthy long-term prison siphoning the fruits of labor from working people and trapping the rest into dependence, doing injustice to both groups in the process.

Recent History of Democrats' War on the Poor

Lyndon Johnson's "War on Poverty" began in 1964. It was supposed to give poor people a "hand up, not a hand out." In the 50 years after its introduction, taxpayers were made to spend $22 trillion on this "war." What have Americans who footed the bill gotten in return? Virtually nothing. The poverty rate in 2013 was 14.5 percent, essentially the same as the rate in 1967 when the program began. And, rather than helping the poor become self-sufficient, the "war" has pushed masses of people into dependency while erecting barriers to prevent them from later escaping. Welfare programs discourage work and disincentivize marriage, both factors leading away from self-sufficiency and into increased child poverty.[1]

Elitist and Cold-Hearted

Despite their rhetoric, Democrats' indifference to the plight of poor people is obvious on the topics of school choice and parental rights. Legislative initiatives to enable people of ordinary income to escape public schools are regularly blocked by Democrats. And Democrats benefit from kids in lower income areas remaining trapped in a generational cycle of dependence and crime. At the same time, Democrats' hold a stranglehold monopoly on public schools and sweet crony financial and political arrangements with teachers' unions and other inside operators. Democrats have transformed public schools into leftist political indoctrination mills, and keeping larger numbers of kids down, uninformed, and dependent on government serves Democrat political interests. These factors are the real point, no matter how many times Democrats repeat the mantra "do it for the children."

Dehumanizing

Whether abortion mills, or solicitation of illegal immigration and dangerous border crossings, or "right to die" legislation, or gun control, or opposition to free markets, Democrat policies share one thing in common: They reduce the value of human lives. At the root of their cynical behavior, I believe, is a wrong view of the value of people. Democrats can treat people as disposable because they tend to believe that people are ultimately mere animals. And, if you hold this view, you can treat them differently than you would individuals of worth, each one made in the image of God.

Can Government Be Compassionate?

There is an important place for compassion in society, and the American people are among the kindest and most generous in the world.[2] Driving America's generous spirit are American conservatives, who far outpace all other groups in terms of giving to those in need.[3]

Democrats and the American left (who are also uniformly among the least generous members of American society)[4] regularly make the mistake of asserting that government should be compassionate, and underlying that claim is a careless assumption that government *can* be compassionate. The first assertion, however, is false, because the second is generally impossible—as will be explained below.

Apart from clemency offered by a judge or a governor or a president on an individual, case-by-case basis and hopefully in a manner that does not deny justice to victims of a crime, compassion is *not the business of government*. Why? It is because government must be *fair*, it has a duty to act for the good of the people and, above all, government must not actively perpetrate injustice.

Democrats today are increasingly aligned with George Soros' crusade to install district attorneys that push to shield people from the consequences of their crimes. In some Democrat-governed jurisdictions, people who steal less than $1000 need fear no prosecution. Domestic abusers go unpunished. And so on. Victims of robbery or domestic abuse immediately see the problem: Such policies deny justice to those who deserve it. Also, future potential victims are owed the deterrence that serious consequences for present crimes will carry. When there is no punishment, victimization crime increases, and many are harmed.

It is impossible to be compassionate using other people's money without their consent, and the U.S. government has no money of its own with which to help anyone. If my heart goes out to a needy person and I give some money from my own pocket, that is compassion. But if I snatch the purse of a passerby and split the money between myself and the one in need, I would not be compassionate—I'd be a thief. And that is why the U.S. government has no business showing compassion. Politicians who make a big show of using taxpayer dollars to "help" people are frauds. If they really cared, they would reach into their own pockets, and invite others to do the same. But taking money by force from some Americans and giving it to others is cowardly and dishonest.

Government "Compassion" Hurts The Social Fabric

Beyond being immoral, government "compassion" is harmful to society in at least two important ways. Think of the good feeling you had when you made a charitable gift to someone who could do nothing to help you. Your good feeling came because you did something kind. It is healthy for us to regularly engage in generosity, because doing so strengthens our sense of our common bond as humans and reinforces the fabric of our moral society.

Now, think of the good feeling you had when you sent money to the IRS. Never had that feeling? It is because you did it under compulsion. It was not voluntary. And the mere fact that such programs exist, and you are funding them, hardens your heart in your next encounter with a person who has fallen on hard circumstances. If you do give, it feels like you are paying double, while some fat cat in government enjoys job security, great benefits, and the promise of an early retirement as a pat on the back for having been so "compassionate" with your tax dollars.

Next, think of a time you worked really hard and then got paid for it. It felt good, right? The first part of the Fourth Commandment is "six days you shall labor and do all your work" (Exodus 20:9). We, being made in the image of God, are created to work. And, just as God saw his work at the end of the days of creation and took joy in it, so we experience joy at the fruit of our labors. Pulling people away from work by merely giving them income taken from others deprives those people of a very important part of life, the satisfaction of labor.

This is not the way it should be. Government spending should be for general benefit (such as public parks and roads, or national defense), not for specific benefit of individuals... and particularly not in pursuit of political entrenchment of those who support such programs.

---

1. Robert Rector, "The War on Poverty: 50 years of failure," Heritage Foundation, September 23, 2014.

2. Erica Pandey, "America the generous: U.S. leads globe in giving," Axios, March 12, 2022; Leslie Albrecht, "The U.S. is the No. 1 most generous country in the world for the last decade," Market Watch, December 7, 2019.

3. Arthur C. Brooks, *Who Really Cares? America's Charity Divide: Who Gives, Who Doesn't, and Why It Matters*, (New York: Basic Books, 2006).

4. Ibid.

3

DEPRAVED

No political party or organization has a monopoly on bad morals, and all humans are sinful. That having been said, there is a difference between those who recognize right from wrong and generally speak well of what's right, and those who do not. And finally, some work actively to uproot what's good and to establish that which is evil. The Bible refers to them when it says, "Woe to those who call evil good and good evil" (Isaiah 5:20).

At the time of this writing, Democrats at national and local levels are doing, defending, or in cases even celebrating all of the following:

- theft, including income redistribution
- destruction of property by burning, looting, and defacing
- wholesale lawbreaking, with culprits going free and victims often blamed
- murder of school children (e.g., the 2023 Nashville massacre)

- threatening the lives of judges and their families to influence a decision
- violence against people standing in the way of Democrat political priorities
- all manner of sexual depravity and public vulgarity
- mocking or even attacking attempts at virtue
- teaching children to judge others by the color of their skin
- presentation of inappropriate books such as those showing how to engage in oral and anal sex with adults to children as young as elementary age
- irreversible surgical mutilation of minor children via mastectomies, removal of reproductive organs, or other (so-called) "sex change" operations
- elective abortion
- post-birth murder of a child

If you are inclined toward some of the things listed above, please understand that my listing them does not mean I "hate" you. See again "Your Life Matters" at the beginning of this book. My purpose is to call attention to the moral weight of the items listed.

Multiple U.S. political parties may defend immoral acts among consenting adults—even while acknowledging them to be immoral—in the name of liberty; for example, libertarians might support opportunity for abortion and sexually immoral acts between consenting adults as personal choices that ought to be protected. They reason that adults can choose to expose themselves to harm, so long as they are willing to take personal responsibility for the consequences. However, the wholesale *defense* and even *celebration* of immorality on such a vast array of points as listed above (and even this list is incomplete) is today really localized within the Democratic Party.

Moral relativism is the idea that there is no real right and wrong. Relativists propose that right and wrong are merely societal constructs, meaning that there is nothing inherently right or wrong about them, but people only consider them right or wrong based upon mutual agreement within their own society or culture. And if God does not exist, then they are correct. Aside from the big question of whether moral relativism is in fact true, there arises a major problem: If truth is relative, how can racism, rape, slavery, murder of children, genocide, and other such things, be wrong? By what token, if cultural concensus is the highest authority, can one even say that the murder of six million Jewish men, women, and children, was wrong?

Consequences

Our actions—whether good or bad—bear fruit, and long patterns of action bear very consistent fruit. The fruit of our actions are rarely confined to the individual who does the action. When a man is unfaithful to his wife, he unleashes a chain of harm not only to himself, but also to her, to their children, their friends and community, and so forth. And these consequences can ripple onward for years, even generations. Now, obviously there is going to be sin in the world and we are all going to do wrong things. But when a significant portion of people begin to celebrate what is morally wrong, while blaming and rejecting what is morally right, the effects upon a society that accepts such things will not be avoided.

Democrats today defend all moral choices, except those

they don't happen to like, in the name of "diversity" and "inclusion." They defend corruption and laugh at anyone who speaks up about it or tries to stop it. They oppose people who suggest truth exists. They express selective and arbitrary moral outrage, demanding that we "believe all women" while refusing to even say what a woman is.

Legislating Morality, Spreading Emptiness

Democrats today are legislating their morality, seeking to impose it upon everyone. Unsatisfied with the First Amendment, they insist that people be forced to speak words that Democrats prefer, passing laws and suing those who refuse. They infiltrate companies and institute HR policies to eject employees who don't toe the line. Teachers are fired for refusing to lie to their students.

The idea of a law enforcing morality is not wrong. We have laws against murder and robbery. The problem comes when a law affirms immorality, or requires an act of injustice to be done. The laws "you shall murder" and "you shall not murder" carry opposite moral weight.

Democrats are morally adrift. And they are imposing their confusion and their pain upon the entire nation. They fail to understand that the nation that does what is right will prosper, while the one embracing injustice will descend into even greater injustice and misery. Everyone, even the immoral individual, reaps a blessing when morality is generally affirmed in a nation and held as a standard, even if not perfectly realized all the time.

4

ANTI-SCIENCE

I don't accept "science" from people who claim a man can
be a woman.

— INTERNET MEME, UNATTRIBUTED

The Democratic party today claims that "Climate
change is a global emergency."[1] Prominent Democrats regularly insinuate that removal of guns from
public spaces will make those spaces safer. In the area of
economics, Democrats argue that minimum wage laws and
progressive taxation schemes will help people and the economy. Democrats who express concern about the influence of
money in politics berate others as "not following the science"
if they question research studies funded by government that
recommend an increase in government size and power. All of
these are examples of the anti-science culture within the
Democratic Party.

Although Democrats' rejection of an evidence-based
approach to reality had been noted by astute observers for

decades, the matter came to full public attention in 2020-2021 during the COVID-19 pandemic and its aftermath, and was underscored by the behavior of the party in respect to the so-called transgender movement which came into full flower in 2022. As with the other chapters of this book, my discussion is merely a summary.

What Is Science?

Humans are prone to jump to conclusions. The scientific method is a process for learning about the world and universe as it really is. It is designed to confirm whether how things appear at first glance is actually the way things are. It requires the willingness to follow truth wherever it leads. It also involves stopping where the evidence stops. A good scientist is *humble* and rejects dogma in scientific matters. A scientist must have the ability to think critically and does not claim that something is proven until it is actually demonstrated by experiments that have accounted for all possible variables and sources of error. Sometimes scientific discovery has a useful purpose, and sometimes it does not. Life-saving drugs, the combustion engine, the light bulb, photography, air and space travel, and computers exist today because of scientific discoveries.

The scientific method is only sound to the extent that it is followed with competence, with rigor, and above all with honesty. Any research process that protects and always affirms the funders' personal beliefs, preferences, or financial interests, while ridiculing or uncritically dismissing serious challenges, is not science. Truth twisted is not science. Half-truths lacking context are not science. Suppression of contrary evidence is not science. Tampering with data to bolster a preferred conclusion is absolutely not science.

Because science and its results carry authority, science or the aura of science is an attractive tool for politicians. When they seek to advance a particular policy or law, pointing to a respected study or group of studies supporting the proposal can help them win the argument. Everyone *wants* to claim that science supports their view of the world and how things should be done, so there is a market for scientific studies supporting those things the politicians already want to do. When politicians appeal to "the science," therefore, we should exercise healthy skepticism.

Democrats claim to be the party of science. They are not. For Democrats, I have noted that science serves one ultimate purpose: The increase, centralization, and extension of government power in the pursuit of their own interests. Look at their history. Virtually any research threatening Democrat priorities such as growth of government, increase in government regulations, creation of a new agency or increase of funding or staffing in an old one, ceding power to international bodies, enrichment of major Democrat donors such as unions, the removal of guns from the hands of private citizens, attacks on the institution of marriage, exposure of children to explicit material, affirmation of gender dysphoria, increases in illegal immigration, or hampering of crime prevention, will be ignored, rejected, and even ridiculed by Democrats. Often they even attack the character and competence of anyone who dares support such work.

Democrats don't want science, they want a pretext for domination. They hate scientific discovery when it does not feed their appetite for power and money.

Precommitments Pose A Risk

A conflict of interest exists when someone has a situation in their life with potential to critically cloud their judgment. Conflicts of interest are everywhere in the scientific world. Scientists are human beings just like anyone else, with cares, concerns, occasional political preferences, bills to pay, and families to feed. And, the existence of a conflict of interest is not an insurmountable barrier, so long as there are safe-guards in place to counterbalance the conflict. The biggest conflict of interest in the scientific world today is that of *government funding*. Neutrality of research conducted with the help of government funds is a myth. Government-funded research is extremely vulnerable to agendas that have nothing to do with the dispassionate pursuit of knowledge.

How can we be confident that government-funded research is biased? Just look at the outcomes. Consider this question: When in your lifetime have you ever heard of a scientific research outcome funded by government resulting in a conclusion that further growth of government is not needed? Or that further government intervention in a given problem via the creation of a new agency or program, the expansion of an existing one, or the creation of a new law or regulation, or the affirmation of an existing government law or program is not warranted? When have you heard of a government-funded research study supporting the sunset or elimination of any government agency or program? I am fairly certain that your answer will be the same as mine: Never, or nearly never. We do not see a government-funded study suggesting that the EPA is no longer needed. We do not see a government-funded study indicating that 'climate change' is not a significant problem needing government action, increased taxation, or the hiring of more people into government service. We do not see a government-funded research indicating that less centralized decision-making is better in public schools, or that the elimination of the Department of Education would better serve the nation and its children. Why? Because those in government want research affirming their own existence and growth.[2]

But wait, you might say, Republicans benefit from government too. Why wouldn't the dynamic above apply to Republicans as well as Democrats? The answer is that everyone is biased. The Republican establishment often falls victim to the allure of junk science as well. But despite this, Republicans more often align with actual science for one major reason: Republicans generally inhabit the world *as it is*. Republican policies tend to account for and reflect those things that are supported empirically. Many of these policies and positions came to be originally embraced by the Republican Party *because of* the fact that they were empirically supported. Science was not an afterthought; it was the foundation. So, Republicans generally do not need to twist the science in order to make it fit their policy preferences.

Peer Review

The peer review process is designed to maximize integrity of published research, but it can also be a vehicle for distortion if the peers happen to share unscientific precommitments, conflicts of interest, or bias. When the community of scientists have a political agenda and begin to gang up against or exclude those whose research does not reinforce the objectives of that agenda, there is a big problem. Unfortunately, what is called "science" today is increasingly tainted by such concerns.

Let's turn now to a brief discussion of some examples of issues in which Democrats regularly reject science in order to advance their personal preferences and interests.

Climate

Democrats have by now taken it as given that human-caused climate change has been demonstrated. In this those who truly believe are at their most gullible, while those who do not but act as though they do treat the rest of us as though we were fools.

This book is not the place to make a full presentation or to dig into the studies. I shall be happy to defend my general assertions in another venue. Rather, I present some general observations.

First, time and again over the past sixty years, the American left have tried to foist their climate alarmism upon the populace. The results when many bought into their caterwauling have been dreadful. From Rachel Carson's *Silent Spring* until now, climate alarmism has been an effective tool in the hands of careless scientists and opportunistic politicians to amass wealth and power, and push forward increases in government control and global socialism.

Global disaster caused by sloppy science is nothing new. Thomas Malthus got the ball rolling with his 1798 book *An Essay on the Principle of Population*. Malthus misjudged earth's carrying capacity, leading him to predict catastrophe. Of course, when carrying capacity is reached, there will be a constriction of population. However, we have not come near that point yet.

When I was a child in the 1970s, I recall frightful warnings of a coming ice age. In fact, the fearmongering fluctuates back and forth. First it is global cooling, then global warming, and today it is "climate change."

If you were to survey Democrat elected officials today, you would find that the significant majority will claim that human-caused "climate change" is scientifically proven. It is not, and I doubt that you would find any careful scientist not funded by a government grant who would make such a sweeping statement. The absurdity of such a claim is (ironically) perhaps one of the most outrageous examples of how unscientific many Democrats really are.

Guns

20 US states allow teachers to be armed. In such schools, 'There has yet to be a single person wounded or killed in a shooting, let alone a mass public shooting.' (Lott, 2019)

That's right: 100% of school mass shootings have occurred in schools that are 'gun free.' Zero have occurred in schools that are not.

Given that the above facts are readily available, and Democrats know them very well, the question becomes: Why do Democrats fight tooth and nail to make public schools into 'gun free' zones? It seems to me that there are three possible answers: 1) Democrats simply don't care about kids, 2) Democrats know the facts but have decided that there is some larger objective more important than the short-term protection of children, or there are alternate strategies to protect schools without affirming the societal benefits of gun rights, or 3) Democrats reject empiricism and are anti-science. I believe the truth includes a combination of these three factors, but I absolutely believe—particularly given Democrats' rejection of empiricism on so many of the other issues discussed here—that the anti-science culture is a critical aspect when it comes to gun policy. It is as simple as this: Democrats set gun policy by emotion resting upon careless research, not science. Facts don't matter.

Would you send your kids into one of the most likely places for a mass shooting to occur? Thanks to the perverse reasoning of Democrats, Loudoun public schools are exactly such places, and any parent of LCPS children are doing just that every day.

Unfortunately, there exist many public schools across the nation that today are such dangerous 'gun free' zones. This fact is despite school boards knowing that nearly 98% of all mass shootings, and fully 100% of school mass shootings, in the US have occurred in 'gun free' zones.

There is something wrong with any policy maker who cares more about optics and public opinion than the safety of kids.

Sex and Life

From the moment of conception, humans with XY, XXY, or XYY chromosomes at the 23rd pair are male, and those with XX or XXX are female. Each of the trisomy variations (XXX, known as Trisomy X; XXY, known as Klinefelter syndrome; and XYY, known as Jacob's syndrome) occur in approximately one out of a thousand female or male live births, respectively. These are natural, they may result in certain traits such as acne or increased height, and many people never know that they have the condition.

The genetic information determining sex is present at the

moment of conception. The sex chromosome is duplicated throughout every one of the approximately thirty trillion cells in a person's body. Never in history has anyone's sex been documented to change after the moment of conception.

Yet, Democrats for the most part reject these facts, replacing them with two dogmas. The first is that of gender fluidity and is exemplified by their religious mantra "sex assigned at birth." The second, a mystical assertion that no child is alive until some point after birth, is exemplified by their insistence that laws protecting unborn children affect only the woman's body and nothing more. It is marked by liturgical statements such as "life begins at birth."

Bullying and suicide prevention programs

Presentation of suicide as a way to get back at those who have hurt you, or the naming and glorification of individuals who took their own lives, are known to increase suicide rates among others—particularly youth—who may be struggling with suicidal thoughts. Yet, the book and movie *13 Reasons Why* (2007) was pushed by the Left. The fictional story glorified a girl who took her own life and dramatized the regret of those who became aware of the role they had played in her trauma through her "reasons" left behind for others to discover.

Suicide rates in the U.S. were hovering at or under 11.0 per 100,000, but increased steadily from 2007 onward, reaching a peak of 14.2 per 100,000 in 2018.[3]

Wondering about a link between the suicide rates and the *13 Reasons Why* book and movie seems reasonable, even though the statistics were probably multi-factorial. My observation is more about the uncritical embrace of "doing something" that made people feel good even though evidence suggested it would cost more lives.

Economics

The laws of economics are not the same as those that are empirically verified in chemistry or physics or mathematical proofs, but economics are based upon a tremendous amount of data and experience. We cannot deal with the matter at length here, but to observe that, as with so many other topics, Democrats advance economic policies in pursuit of ideological goals that have little or nothing to do with the purported empirically expected results. The enormous success of free market capitalism, everywhere it has ever been employed, in creating a rising tide that lifts all boats, is as undeniable as is the absolute failure of Communism everywhere it has ever been implemented. However, to Democrats the fact that some boats may get lifted higher than others—even though the others are rising too—is emotionally unacceptable and causes them to reject reason in favor of policies that harm everyone. Spite, in other words, overrides reason.

COVID-19: Vaccines, Masks, and More

Democrats' rejection of science was seen as clearly as ever during the events of 2020 and 2021 during the COVID-19 pandemic. The nation was divided and Democrats even became violent over the matter of mask wearing, even outdoors, despite it being admitted in the May 2020 issue of the *New England Journal of Medicine* that masks were "marginally beneficial" in preventing the spread of COVID.[4] Meanwhile, draconian and overbearing lockdowns pushed by wild-eyed Democrats needlessly destroyed small businesses and cost millions of Americans their jobs, or even their lives through depression and suicide, while school closures harmed children with learning loss at a crucial stage of development that in many cases will never be recovered.[5] That there was no scientific basis for the extreme shutdowns, and much less for the type of universal vaccination that the Democrats were pushing, was observed by many reasonable people. However, such people were met with vicious, scathing, and often violent vitriol from Democrats.

Other Examples of Democrat Anti-Science Stances

At the top of this short chapter, I mentioned some examples of Democrat dogmas that exhibit an anti-scientific approach to knowledge. Let us mention two more, and then conclude. Many Democrats classify CO_2, one of the most abundant compounds on earth without which abundance plant life could not survive, as a pollutant. While anything can be a pollutant if it does not belong somewhere, it is nonsensical to call CO_2 a pollutant in the atmosphere of planet earth, where the compound is naturally occurring and an essential part of the respiration process. Second, many Democrats still subscribe to the notion that there is what they call a "gender pay gap," by which they seem to mean a sex pay gap. Neither have been shown to exist, as was brought out in the now-famous 2018 interview between Jordan Peterson and Cathy Newman, in which he demonstrated that if you properly account for variables, among other things, no pay gap exists and, if anything, women might earn slightly more than men for the same work.[6]

Magical Thinking

Underlying Democrats' troubled relationship with science is a general habit of sloppy thinking. Democrats so often seem to expect that good intentions will solve problems, or that doing the same thing that failed the last ten times will somehow render a different result if tried again. This is careless. It is wishful thinking. And there is no excuse for it when it comes to matters of public policy that have real life consequences. Not all public policy needs to be grounded in an airtight scientific study, but policies ought to follow rational thought based upon past experience and a critical evaluation of the available evidence.

---

1. "Combating the climate crisis and pursuing environmental justice," *democrats.org*,

2. Obviously, we would expect *some* portion of neutral research to support expansion of a program or other government priority. What we should not expect is that neutral research would *always* support the expansion or maintenance of the status quo adn pre-determined policy preferences of the bureaucrats.

3. "Suicide Data and Statistics," Centers for Disease Control and Prevention.

4. Michael Klompas et al., "Universal Masking in Hospitals in the Covid-19 Era," *New England Journal of Medicine*, May 21, 2020. 2020; 382:e63.

5. "Levin: This is a massive coverup," Fox News, March 5, 2023. https://www.youtube.com/watch?v=ejCrrr9L69k

6. "Jordan Peterson debate on the gender pay gap, campus protests and postmodernism," Channel 4 News, January 16, 2018. https://youtu.be/aMcjxSThD54

5

MISOGYNIST

As we have already mentioned, Democrats today have trouble even defining what a woman is. That is to say, they *can't even see* women. Given this situation, it should come as no surprise that such lack of clarity would lead them to roll over women and do them harm. In my observation, Democrats expect women—like so many other unfavored groups—to stand aside in order to make way for a Democrat agenda that is more important than the concerns of women for fairness, opportunity, and recognition.

Democrats, to be sure, do not have a monopoly when it comes to harming women. The problem of mysogyny, as the problem of racism discussed in Chapter 1, is a result of our human sinfulness and can be found across all superficial barriers. As with the racism problem, so also here injustice follows a failure to recognize women as made in the image of God (Genesis 1:27). However, when it comes to harming women, Democrats are leading the way and have done so for a very long time.

Tokens

What is womens' major purpose in the eyes of Democrats? By watching events of the past several years, one might reasonably conclude that it is merely to make Democrats look good. Kamala Harris was chosen as a running-mate by Joe Biden not for her character or qualifications, but because she is a "woman of color." Next, Biden chose Ketanji Brown Jackson for the Supreme Court not for her qualifications—at least not as a primary concern—but because she is a "woman of color." The irony of both these cases is the unwillingness of Democrats, and in the latter instance even the nominee herself, to define what a woman is.

But women are individuals, with particular aspirations, hopes, and desires. Many individual women are more capable than men in many different areas of competence. Our oldest daughter recently met the first U.S. female fighter pilot. In addition to many roles considered more traditional, women today are doctors, engineers, lawyers, CEOs, plumbers, and mechanics. What is it about women that makes Democrats seem to only see their sex and other physical traits?

The Democrat Campaign To Erase and Expose Women

And then, what is it about women that makes Democrats not recognize them as unique at all, even declaring that a man can be a better woman than a woman? On international women's day, 2023, the Biden White House chose to honor Argentinian Alba Rueda, who is male.[1]

Women in many parts of the world, including the United States, have long struggled to be seen, understood, acknowledged. In the U.S., women made great progress in the work-place over the last forty years. It is no longer unusual to see women holding positions formerly dominated by men. Today a greater percentage of U.S. adults with a bachelors' degree are women, and the gap is widening. Our oldest daughter, Rivka, will soon be commissioned as an officer in the Space Force, and my wife is a vice president at a $2B medical company, overseeing about one-sixth of that business. Our second daughter, Avigail, is pursuing biomedical engineering and archaeology. None of these accomplishments devalues the work of women who devote themselves fully to home-making, child rearing, or home schooling roles. My point is that there is liberty and opportunity in the United States for every individual person and family to make their own decisions.

In the midst of this encouraging situation, Democrats stepped up to deny women—apparently—even the right to exist. Using the "transgender" movement as an excuse, Democrats became cheerleaders for a complete erasure of womanhood into utter nonsensical meaninglessness. They've denied the scientific reality of sex, pretending it does not exist, and in so doing have effectively eliminated men from their lexicon as well.

While, certainly, both men and women have suffered from this maneuver, women bore most of the harm. In a world that pretends human sexual dimorphism (that is, the general differentiation of the sexes in various traits including strength) does not exist when in fact it does, males will have an advantage and females will be unable to compete at the highest levels in many areas, especially sports. For this reason, mediocre male athletes began setting records imme-diately upon entry into womens' sports, pushing the ceiling

out of reach for actual women at the very moment when
society was establishing a robust and meaningful structure of
recognition and achievement for women in many of these
sports.

Furthermore, when women protest against the injustice,
they are viciously attacked...by Democrats. "Riley Gaines, a 12
time All-American swimmer with 5 SEC titles...was forced to
share a locker room and then compete against biological
male Lia Thomas at the 2022 NCAA Women's Swimming
Championship."[2] The two tied in the women's 200-yard
freestyle event down to the hundredth of a second, but
NCAA officials gave Thomas the trophy. Victories by males in
women's sports events began to occur immediately as
Democrats pushed for the erasure of sex distinctions in these
events. In 2021, Joe Biden gutted Title IX, the 1972 law that
was passed to *prevent* sex discrimination in education, by
removing its protections of female athletes from sex discrimination by having to compete against men.[3]

But it gets worse. The "gender identity" cult was quickly
seized upon by opportunistic men who used it as a vehicle to
rape and impregnate women. Male prison inmates strate-
gized to "identify" as women and were granted transfer to
women's prisons, raping the existing inmates. In 2022, 27-
year-old male, Demi Minor, who claimed to be transgender,
impregnated two female inmates at the Garden State Youth
Correctional Facility, a prison for women aged 18 to 30.[4]

Democrats' devaluation of women also appears in other
aspects of Democrat policy and action, perhaps nowhere
more prominently than in Democrats' position on guns. A
gun is a tool that can give its bearer—even one who is much
smaller or weaker—an advantage over an unarmed opponent, or equalizes the situation in an encounter with an

armed attacker. Few people benefit more from freedom to keep and bear arms than women. In places where the carry of firearms is permitted, victimization crimes against women plummet. This trend occurs whether or not any given woman is actually carrying a firearm. The mere possibility is typically enough to dissuade potential attackers from taking the chance.

Drag

In 2022, 25-year-old actor Dylan Mulvaney announced his intention to transition his gender. Immediately, Mulvaney began dressing, speaking, and acting as though trying to play the part of an exaggerated and cartoonish version of a giddy pre-teen girl. He continued mocking girls in this way for at least the next year, amassing fortune and tremendous fame. But since his behavior fed a Democrat pet cause, Mulvaney was exempt from criticism by leftist elites. Observed Billy Bragg, "If Mr Mulvaney was getting rich by pretending to be black and exploiting degrading stereotypes about black people for 'comedy' no one would deny they could see the problem. It is only women who are told to accept, and indeed celebrate, their degradation."[5] Noted one internet meme: "Drag is to women what blackface is to Black people: a costume, a caricature, a mockery, a cheapening, a dehumanization." A Loudoun County, Virginia mom wrote more generally of the transgender and drag phenomena, "Women are being erased by the very clowns who claim to be 'pro-woman.' Womanhood is not a costume, and biology is not bigotry."[6] Yet, Democrats were all-in. Alexandria Ocasio Cortez became a judge on Ru Paul's "Drag Race," and Nancy Pelosi later appeared on the show as well.

The History: Suffrage

Democrats have in recent decades styled themselves as the party of women. The truth throughout history is somewhat less favorable. Republicans drove the movement for women's suffrage, with Senator A.A. Sargent (R) introducing the 19th Amendment at the request of Susan B. Anthony in 1878. The amendment was defeated four times by a Democrat controlled Senate, only passing once Republicans retook control in 1919. But that was not the end of the battle, since a constitutional amendment needs ratification by three-quarters of the state legislatures. Of the 36 states that ratified, 26 had Republican legislatures. Eight of the nine states that voted *against* ratification had Democratic legislatures.[7]

The first woman elected to Congress was Republican Jeannette Rankin in 1919. Republican Ronald Reagan appointed Sandra Day O'Connor, the first female associate justice of the U.S. Supreme Court, in 1981.

---

1. Alexander Hall, "Twitter laughs, groans as Jill Biden gives biological male Woman of Courage award: 'Up your game, ladies,'" *Fox News*, March 8, 2023.
2. "Swimming Against The Current." https://rileygaines.com/?amp=1
3. Collin Binkley, "Biden admin extends Title IX protections to transgender students," *PBS*, June 16, 2021.
4. Tat Bellamy-Walker, "N.J. trans prisoner who impregnated 2 inmates transferred to men's facility," *NBC News*, July 19, 2022.
5. Billy Bragg, tweet, April 9, 2023.
6. Elizabeth Boyko, Facebook post, March 9, 2023. Quoted with permission.
7. "Suffrage," National Federation of Republican Women. https://nfrw.org/women-suffrage

GASLIGHTERS AND DECEIVERS

W hen abusers and bullies get caught in the act, they often deflect attention and blame others, including their victims. People who aren't doing bad things don't need to hide or deflect attention in this way.

From the time of slavery until the present moment, Democrats have embraced bad principles. In years past, they were able to be more open about their support for slavery and racism. Today, they couch their beliefs and actions in jargon, while trying to revise history and obfuscate truth on all manner of topics. It is utterly dishonest.

The Language Game

Language is the battlefield where much of Democrats' war on truth is being waged. There are many examples, but one most current at the time of this writing is the subtle shift mentioned at the conclusion of the previous chapter: blurring the relationship between physical reality and personal belief or preference.

Democrats' habitual substitution of the term "gender" for the word "sex" muddies the linguistic waters. Gender is a term of grammar, that carries a *sense* of sex but absent a necessary connection to it. In Germany, as everywhere in the world, there are two human sexes (male and female), but in the German language there are three genders (masculine, feminine, and neuter) which are assigned to their objects by convention. Chairs, apples, and cars have no sex, but they do have grammatical genders in German. Since disruption of the link between language and physical reality is their goal, Democrats have substituted the word "gender" for sex. It is their attempt to escape the reality that nobody has ever changed their sex, in order to craft an illusion that everything is fluid.

Since we already have words for sex (male and female), it makes little sense to speak of "gender" in reference to people, unless one intends to refer to something *other* than sex. The word "gender" is arbitrary, but sex is not. By conflating the two, Democrats set the stage for all sorts of harm.

"We're Not Teaching CRT"

Democrats in classrooms, on school administrations, and school boards across the country, even in very conservative states,[1] lie to parents and citizens about their pedagogies and educational content. I have experienced it in my home of Loudoun County, as our schools became a spectacle to the outside world. When confronted, Democrats obfuscate by shifting language, but keep the racist and marxist content.

In 2021, most Democrats in my state insisted that Critical

Race Theory (CRT) was not being taught or its pedagogy implemented in Virginia public schools. Did Democrats believe their line? Of course not! Furthermore, they are huge fans of CRT, because it advances their core conviction that race defines the human being and that some races are superior to others. The problem for Democrats is that most Americans do not embrace that idea, and even many regular Democrats know they can't support it publicly. So, they ridicule and accuse those asking questions of imagining things, being paranoid, and being way too sensitive. But it is they who are the liars. The following admissions were caught on hidden camera by an investigator for the Daily Signal. I have not confirmed that all the people quoted are Democrats, but it is quite reasonable to assume.

Tracey Noe, Assistant Superintendent in Goshen, Indiana admitted, "We did tweak the name of our equity and inclusion committee...because we just didn't want to make a target of it...and so, we renamed it, but that's the work we do." Asked what she renamed it, she said, "Right now, it's named a 'work group' [laughs]."[2]

Dr. Laura DelVecchio, Assistant Superintendent in Plainfield, Indiana, asked whether they still have an equity department, said, "So, honestly, so...what we've decided to do is not call attention to it, because when you call attention to it, then questions are asked, and I really believe that you can do more good under the radar." She also said, "Right before COVID, we had started some really deep diving into our curriculum and kind of doing that, like, white privilege walk and making sure, like, just, understand, right?" DelVecchio mentioned "pride" posters in classrooms, and said they tell the teachers to just "be subtle," stating, "We really, like, we stay under the radar. And we'd like to keep it that way. [laughs]"[3]

Terri L. Roberts-Leonard, Equity and Inclusion officer in Carmel, Indiana, said, "Each of our fifteen schools has an equity and inclusion team in their building. And then, each school has a rep that they send to the district teams. So that's how we try to, like, build capacity...it's interwoven into the fabric of what we do."[4]

Jenny Oakley, Director of e-learning & Literacy in Martinsville, Indiana, tells of the district's collusion with textbook companies to sneak subversive materials into their books while avoiding key words that might draw attention: "We talked about, to our textbook companies...and I actually prep them a little bit because I'm like, 'We want this in our curriculum, so if you could just not say specifically this, then it won't cause a red flag with the community.' I hate that we have to do that, but that way, it's still there."[5]

When asked about "social and emotional learning," Brad Sheppard, Assistant Superintendent in Elkhart, Indiana said, "Yeah, it has become a bad phrase. And we don't openly use that phrase, but we're still doing it."[6]

The deception and withholding of information from parents exposes children to danger of assault. Debra Prenkert, Director of Elementary Education in Monroe, Indiana, tells about elementary school trips to Bradford Woods: "They used to have boy cabin and girl cabin, and we're like, 'Well, where do they want to identify?' Or you know, I mean, they can say where they feel most comfortable...sometimes I get parents that aren't thrilled with some of the decisions we make. But, that's what we believe in, you know. We're really about equity for all kids."[7]

Deceptive Repackaging

Newsela, a curriculum service that partners with the New York Times' racist 1619 Project, the Southern Poverty Law Center, and supportive of the work of the late radical leftist Howard Zinn, is used as a trojan horse to get such content into public schools. Newsela repackages 1619 Project content while avoiding that name and replacing the New York Times' name with its own, Newsela. Asked about whether Newsela partners with the Southern Poverty Law Center, Howard Zinn, and so forth, Monica Kegerrels, Assistant Superintendent of Fairfield, Indiana, said, "Yes. Now, our teachers know that. They're not saying that out loud. OK, does that make sense? [laughs] Semantics. [laughs]"[8]

Lying To Teachers In A Push For Unions

Unions are big businesses whose prime interests are making money for the union and advancing the union's power through political advocacy on behalf of those who will give the union more power and money. The National Education Association (NEA) spends $2 on politics for every $1 it spends representing members.[9]

At the moment of writing, the Loudoun Education Association is making a big push to unionize Loudoun County Public Schools. The unions and their shills have been selling the move by saying that teachers deserve a "voice" and a "seat at the table." They have also waved pictures of red herrings, accusing those of us warning that unionization will cost the taxpayers millions of additional dollars per year of lying. Yet, the actual effect of these collective bargaining contracts is to *remove* the teachers' voices by forbidding them from talking to the school administration on topics delineated by the agreement. And, exactly one week after the Democrats on the LCPS board passed the collective bargaining resolution, they submitted a request for an additional $3.3 million to fund thirteen new administrative positions whose sole purpose will be to handle collective bargaining matters. In other words, the Democrats lied to us.

The unions edge their way in, but they make sure to lodge themselves in place so as to make it extremely difficult to remove them. And even though there is a way out, the unions do everything to make it easy to enter but very difficult to leave.[10] And, the teachers unions have been leading the charge in pushing Critical Race Theory in our K-12 schools.[11]

---

1. Tony Kinnett, "Indiana Public School Officials Admit Lying to Parents About Critical Race Theory," Daily Signal, April 17, 2023.
2. "Caught on tape: Indiana administrators are deceiving parents," Accuracy in Media, April 12, 2023. https://youtu.be/QlCVHHXKJWg
3. Ibid.
4. Ibid.
5. Ibid.
6. Ibid.
7. Ibid.
8. Ibid.
9. "How Do Unions Spend Your Dues?" Americans For Fair Treatment.
10. Todd DeFeo, "Ohio public employees win settlement in 'limited window' union dues case," *Washington Examiner*, July 15, 2020.
11. Larry Sand, "It's time to abolish the teachers unions," California Policy Center, December 23, 2021.

TOTALITARIAN

"The opposite of cruelty is freedom. The victim does not need the ultimately destructive gift of kindness when offered *within the cruel relationship.* He needs freedom from that relationship." —Philip Hallie[1]

The Lego Movie (2014) is an allegory for our time. Its root message is that, while some laws are needed, people ought not have every area of their lives managed by external micromanagers. The world is a more beautiful place when people have room to make choices and live their lives in relative freedom—that is, to pursue happiness without constant harassment. Government does not need to run everything, and government is rightly the servant of the people, not their master.

Freedom means having an open range of possibilities, and the opportunity to decide how to navigate the various challenges and opportunities we face. A loved one has cancer, no insurance, and you don't know what to do next? In a free market situation you have options. Some may be expensive. But, you are not without options if your loved one doesn't meet the socialists' criteria for treatment. Those facing such situations in other countries at least have somewhere to go: the United States. And many do so, at least if not prohibited, as were the parents of Charlie Gard in 2017, when the British government (who were going to let the child die and apparently feared the bad press for the NHS if he lived after the proposed treatment in New York) forbade them from taking their child out of the country. The government considered the child's imminent death to be in his "best interest." If we continue down the route Democrats are taking us, there will remain few places to which we can escape when the socialist system inevitably lets us down too.

Why do Democrats object so strongly to freedom with all its risks and potential rewards? The answer is worldview. Democrats tend to embrace materialism, the view that the meaning of life is found in *things*. It explains their support for socialism, welfare, cronyism, forced unionization, and other programs designed to line their own pockets.

The irony of Democrat support for socialism, more regulation, or more government control generally, is that all these *drive up prices*. In healthcare, food, clothing—everything people need. Socialists promise that when you give up freedom, you will get "affordable" healthcare, housing, transportation, college, and so on. It is a lie. Taxes go up, housing costs go up, and the prices you pay at the grocery store, at the gas pump, in property taxes, and online all go up too. Most people don't realize it until it is too late. It's the bitter fruit of greed that comes when people covet that which belongs to their neighbor. It hurts both neighbor and self.

Democrats push to manage the tiniest details of people's lives. They seem to believe that they have a right to tell a shop owner that he is not allowed to give a shopping bag *that the owner paid for personally* to his own customer. Think of this: It is a private interaction not involving drugs, chemical weapons, or any other controlled substance! It is the gift of an item that will make the customer's life a little easier during the trip home. So, perhaps we must now call shopping bags "controlled substances!" Democrats have moved to regulate straws for soft drinks, making plastic straws illegal in favor of paper ones that disintegrate when they come into contact with liquid. In some jurisdictions, Democrats have made it illegal to sell soft drinks in sizes exceeding a certain volume —even if customer and seller both want it. The same goes for light bulbs. And now, even one of the most beautiful appliances in any home, the gas stove.

All these things are examples of incredible, totalitarian overreach that demonstrate the ridiculous absurdities to which Democrats believe they are entitled to get into other people's business. And, we could go down the list: minimum wage, light bulbs, separating garbage. In some states, like California, Democrats have made it illegal for schools to even make their *own* decision to allow handguns to be carried by employees with concealed carry permits. Democrats in many jurisdictions have made it illegal for property owners to charging the actual value in rent.

Encroaching Upon the People's Sovereignty

In the United States, remember, we do not have a king. We are not ruled over. We are a people with a government, not a government with a people. From the time of slavery until the present moment, however, Democrats have always been fond of the idea that some people (i.e., them) should be able to manage the lives of other people in every minute detail. We will address this matter further in the next chapter, but for now it is important to remember, first, that the United States Constitution does not permit the federal government to engage in spending or regulating anything that is not listed in the Tenth Amendment, and second, that the Constitution places all legislative power in Congress.

Today, we are in a constitutional crisis. Your right to govern yourself through your elected representatives is curtailed as Democrats have created all sorts of agencies run by unelected bureaucrats, such as the EPA, that today legislate without your consent. The Department of Education is forbidden by the Constitution, yet it exists as vehicle for turning your own children against you and against the nation, while funneling billions of your tax dollars to unions that push a Democrat political agenda. Meanwhile, honest bakers, florists, wedding venue owners, and others are being sued and run out of town for exercising their First Amendment right to abstain from endorsing activities they consider immoral.

Friends, this is the stuff of totalitarianism, and it is driven, from start to finish, by Democrats.

---

1. Philip Hallie, *The Paradox of Cruelty*, (Middletown: Wesleyan University Press, 1969), 159.

8

SUPPORTERS OF INJUSTICE AND INVOLUNTARY SERVITUDE

Have you ever wondered why socialism has taken root in the Democrat Party, but not in the Republican? It is not a coincidence - it is entirely consistent with the Democrat Party's core philosophy clear back to the time of slavery: *Democrats have no fundamental objection to involuntary servitude, and will always find a way to preserve it in one form or another.*

Supporters of involuntary servitude only get rejected by the Party when they have outlived their usefulness to Democrats' campaign to perpetuate involuntary servitude. Thus, involuntary servitude-supporting Ibram X. Kendi is embraced by the Democrat Party, but he and the Party treat their segregationist and Democrat brother-in-arms Bull Connor as though he is not cut from the same cloth and an ally in the cause.[1] Why? Because overt racism is no longer defensible. Democrats now need to be more subtle.

Democratic socialism is nothing more than an electoral mob that sees fit to conscript some of their neighbors into involuntary servitude.

Prosperity And Opportunity Are Problems For Democrats

On the way to the slavery of socialism, however, there is one major roadblock: Nations with social mobility (meaning a poor person has real opportunities) and a relatively large and content middle class[2] that feels confident in their opportunities for improvement tend to reject wealth redistribution schemes. Understanding this fact will help you to understand many other policies and initiatives of Democrats, who desperately want to eliminate the middle, forcing transfer of most wealth toward an increasingly small group of people (their friends), and pushing a great majority of everyone else into a far more modest—even desperate—financial state. Why? Because doing so prepares the ground for people to vote for help in the form of more government programs.

Understanding this objective of Democrats helps to make sense of their draconian actions during the COVID-19 event. Even though extended shutdowns and extreme disruption of the economy was not warranted, it served the purpose of driving many small businesses to ruin, drain the personal savings of tens of millions of Americans while greatly enriching a few friends of Democrats at the top, and drive millions of regular people into reliance upon government programs.

The Real Purpose of Obamacare

Obamacare was expressly designed to devour the savings of middle- to upper-middle income Americans, driving an ever greater proportion of the nation out of self-sufficiency and into a state of financial desperation that would leave them no choice but to turn to the government for help. It was to do this by forcing a painful increase to the cost of healthcare and health "insurance" for all Americans while at the same time requiring every American to buy this more costly health "insurance." Included with the law was a requirement on all health "insurance" companies that they could not deny anyone on the basis of a pre-existing condition. Obviously, this new rule made it impossible for any private insurer to remain in the business, since customers could avoid signing up until they had a very expensive need, and then they could join up and the health "insurer" would have no choice but to pay out. No true insurance business can operate this way; they would be bankrupt in no time. And that was part of the plan: Obamacare was designed to force these private businesses to become vassals of the federal government, subject to the management and dictates of centralized bureaucracy.

Obamacare itself was not the end goal, it was the first step in a multi-stage process whose intended culmination was the complete transformation of the United States into a socialist society.

Why Democrats Hate Equality

DC-area radio host Chris Plante often quips, "Thank goodness for double standards; if it weren't for double standards, Democrats would have no standards at all." This statement is funny because it is true.

Democrats do not act as though they believe all people are equal or deserve equal treatment. You will be hard pressed to find any Democrat politician today willing to hold illegal immigrants to the same laws as other immigrants. You will find nearly every Democrat supporting "equity" programs to deny students of different races a level playing field in admissions.

A girl in my home of Loudoun County was uncomfortable when a male student came into her bathroom. When the situation was taken to the school administration, she was told that if she was uncomfortable, she could use one of the school's single-use restrooms instead of the girls' restroom. And, she was offered the services of psychological counseling. The rationale given was that the male "has a right to feel safe in the restroom corresponding to their gender identity," or words to that effect. However, even under Joe Biden's creative reading of Title IX, this situation involves *two* protected individuals, yet the school administration only asked the female to bend to accommodate the other student. Was the male directed to use a single-use restroom and offered psychological counseling? Apparently not. And so, a male was favored over a female in a space that is specifically allowed to be separated by sex (separation of spaces by biological sex is expressly protected under Title IX), and the female student probably has a claim of Title IX sex discrimination against the school administration.

Why do Democrats hate equality? I have already discussed some of the reasons above and in Chapter 1. I believe that Democrats also simply feel they should get to make the rules, and everyone else's job is to just say "ok." But they have a broken moral compass.

Theft

Whether you do it yourself or hire someone to do it for you, stealing is wrong. And it doesn't matter whether the victim is poor or rich. The commandment does not say, "You shall not steal...except from rich people." It does not say, "You shall not covet...unless you think the person has too much stuff or is greedy or you don't think they deserve so much." No. It says "You shall not steal" and "You shall not covet."

The Bible forbids favoring either the poor or the rich. "You shall do no injustice in judgment; you shall not be partial to the poor nor defer to the great, but you are to judge your neighbor fairly." (Leviticus 19:15). Everyone deserves justice, and there is no income level at which you become a fair target for theft.

How would you like to be treated if you work hard and finally achieved some financial success? Would you want to be vilified or to have other people feel as though they are entitled to what you've achieved? No. This is the principle that led to the abolition of slavery: People own the fruit of their labor. If they choose, they can sell their labor or its products for a price, and the result (money, for example) is the owner's accumulated residue of that labor. All Americans should take joy in this arrangement, because a society that treats others as they want to be treated is far superior to the alternative.

Denying a person's ownership of himself or herself, and therefore the fruit of his or her labor, is called involuntary servitude, or slavery. Involuntary servitude never fit with the Declaration of Independence and slavery was formally outlawed by passage of the 13th Amendment on January 31, 1865, supported by every Republican in Congress, but only 13 Democrats. Most Democrats opposed the amendment.

Even though involuntary servitude is illegal, Democrats have found ways to preserve it, and its perpetuation remains a core of the Democrat platform today.

Involuntary Servitude

When another person claims the fruits of your labor without your consent, this is involuntary servitude. Simple taxation is not necessarily involuntary servitude because taxation may be laid upon people evenly and its benefits enjoyed by all. However, if property exists—that is, if people can own things —then taxation that redistributes wealth from its owner, against his or her will, to another person is indeed involuntary servitude. Wealth redistribution is, I believe, unconstitutional under the 13th Amendment.

Imagine a scenario. I am in a room with you and a third person. I form an alliance with the third person and the two of us decide we want to take something you own from you, to have for ourselves. However, in the name of "democracy" and "economic justice," we decide not just to seize it from you but to take a vote first. The ballots are counted and—what a surprise—there are two votes in favor of taking your stuff and giving it to myself and my new friend. Hooray! The people have spoken!

Is this justice? No, it is theft. It is upon such theft that Democrats in the United States now rely for their ongoing political success. Democrats feed the covetousness and greed of some people who want to take from their neighbors by force rather than making their way by honest means. It is the heritage of slavery.

A 51% vote does not change truth. The United States were unique in the history of the world for asserting that there are certain rights that every single human being has which cannot be taken away because they come not from government, but from God. Among these rights, the founders said, were life, liberty, and the pursuit of happiness. Property is inseparable from the second of these, derived from the first, and indispensable for the third.

But what about the "greater good?" a Democrat might ask. "Isn't it better that one person or minority group suffer so that society as a whole benefits?" And now you can see how a Democrat thinks, and why the philosophy of the Democrats has not really changed from the 1850s until today. The truth is, Democrats have never really understood nor embraced the proposition that all people have rights.

The simple fact is (and this is the very foundation of the American Experiment), injustice toward any individual never serves the greater good. Remember, Democrats have often made the decision to deny the rights of certain minorities of people in favor of what they saw as the "greater good," for example via the institution of chattel slavery (c. 1620-1864), Jim Crow laws (1877-1964/65), Democrat FDR's internment of Japanese Americans via Executive Order 9066 (1942), and Democrat Barack Obama and all Congressional Democrats' determination that higher income people don't have the right to pay only the market rate for healthcare (2009).

Injustice

Democrats act as though one has the right to expect the same fruit to emerge whether planting weeds or crops. Then, when the same fruit does not emerge, the left blames the farmer that planted crops, seizes their harvest, and gives it to the one who planted weeds. In schools, Democrats excoriate anyone who tries to pull weeds and only plant life-giving and useful crops among our children who are bursting with potential. By weeds and healthy crops I mean the influences and material that are planted in children's minds.

Socialism, which is involuntary servitude, is unjust. Judicial activism, which steals the people's right to have the laws made by their representatives enforced, is unjust. Demonizing wealth inequality is unjust. A graduated taxation system is unjust. Trapping the poor into generational welfare is unjust. A "preferential option for the poor," which applies uneven standards, is unjust. Unequal application of laws, non-application of laws (such as open borders or abolishing ICE) is unjust. A minimum wage infringes the right of private property and is therefore unjust. Allowing fraud by forbidding the checking of voter ID is unjust. Democrats support all these unjust things, and many more.

Mark Of An Abuser: Using The Term "Brother's Keeper"

Democrats love to quote nice-sounding phrases in support of their schemes. The words "brother's keeper" occur in the Bible only once. They were uttered by Cain, who in a fit of anger and jealousy killed his brother Abel and then foolishly tried to hide it from God. Any good Bible student knows that "brother's keeper" is not a good phrase. Nowhere in the Bible does God command anyone to be his "brother's keeper," and anyone who says that they plan to be their "brother's keeper," or expects others to do so, is probably up to no good. Cain did not owe his brother a socialist safety net. Cain owed it to his brother *not to kill him.*

---

1. Kendi, Ibram X., *Stamped: Racism, Antiracism, and You*, New York: Little Brown and Company, 2020.
2. The United States, of course, does not have a class structure, since anyone can and do move between wealth categories, so I employ the term "class" merely for convenience.

9

MARXIST

In July of 2021, the outbreak of protests in Cuba against the nation's communist regime was met with virtual silence from Democrats and the American Left.[1]

There was a time not long ago when any American politician embracing marxism made strenuous attempts to hide or deny it. Now, that mask has been cast aside as it is no longer needed amid the cultural rot that cultural marxism's proponents have cultivated inside the United States in recent years. Today, marxism and Communism are not viscerally rejected by most all Americans as they were even two decades ago.

Re-normalization of sympathy for involuntary servitude, long after the nation rejected it through a costly Civil War and the passage of the 13th Amendment, has been accelerated by the left's seizure of American institutions (e.g., government and education) and by massive expansion of illegal immigration to favor people sympathetic to Communism while amplifying their voices and cultural influence. At this moment, marxists in the United States seem to believe that they are within striking distance of their long-planned dreadful victory: the final enslavement of all Americans to a socialist "utopia."

It should surprise no one that many books and articles today note the marxist commitments of the American Democratic Party. The stark reality of Democrat belief slaps us in the face constantly. The American left, today essentially identical with the Democratic Party, is marxist in its view of the world, premises, and objectives. As with any cancer, there are degrees of infection, but calls for progressive taxation, "affordable housing," and sending "enemies of the people" before a firing squad are all fruits of the same tree at different stages of ripeness.

Democrats' fondness for marxism and the Frankfurt School of economics, both closely associated with the term "progressivism," stretches back toward the time of slavery. It was no coincidence that the Party of Slavery quickly became the Party of Fabian Socialism; the two are twins. Progressivism promotes seizure of the fruits of others' labor while denying human sinfulness. It proposes that people are basically good and can be perfected given the right circumstances and societal conditions. Progressivism, disagreeing with the Bible,[2] and with all of human history and experience, also asserts that economic inequality is immoral and a hindrance to progress. Resisting progressivism requires acknowledgment that people are morally flawed and inclined toward sin, yet have inherent value and rights as individuals. This premise is a defining principle of the conservative side of the American political spectrum.

A form of progressivism defined the slaveholding American South, and it characterized those—even, unfortunately, some who professed Christian faith—who sought to justify the institution of chattel slavery on grounds that it could improve and protect the ones in bondage. Progressives love to speak about what eventually came to be known as "human rights." However, they tend to not understand—and indeed deny—the two essential characteristics of any human right: 1) it is a negative right (see glossary), and 2) that is inherent and unalienable because God-given. God, and therefore rights given by God, are generally foreign to the progressives' materialist view of the universe. For political reasons, progressives sometimes speak as though God exists, but one always finds relativism at the root of progressive rhetoric.

Woodrow Wilson, born and raised in the American South, was elected U.S. President as a Democrat in 1912 and enthusiastically embraced progressivism. Wilson, a racist who demonstrated his fondness for involuntary servitude by warmth to socialism, was the first post-Civil War president to chart a course forward nurturing this new manifestation of the now-defeated official institution of slavery.

Why did the Democratic Party embrace the Frankfurt School? The answer is that the Democratic Party *already embraced* the core assumptions of the marxist/progressive worldview: 1) materialism, 2) involuntary servitude is justifiable, and 3) raw power is ultimately all that matters.

Today, the Democratic Party is entirely compromised by marxism. A very partial list of the standouts include Barack Obama, George Soros, American-born terrorist William Ayers, the late Saul Alinsky, and Joe Biden. But in truth, a majority of elected Democrats today are tainted by marxism. All the named individuals have supported wealth redistribution and a movement toward socialism and centralized government. To the list can be added organizations such as Black Lives Matter and Antifa, both of which are informed by and aligned with a marxist ideology.[3]

Maligning Free Markets

Another sign of Democrats' embrace of marxism is their animosity toward healthy competition and economic freedom. They love to talk about marxist "public-private partnership," "affordable healthcare," "affordable housing," the rich paying their "fair share" (despite the fact that they already pay far more than their fair share), and the dangers of "unrestrained capitalism."

There is no such thing as "unrestrained capitalism." Capitalism is, by definition, the upholding of contracts voluntarily entered. A contract restrains. When contracts are broken, authorities bribed to tolerate injustice, or cronies persuade politicians to legislate so as to harm the competition, these things are not capitalism. To say you favor capitalism but not "unrestrained" capitalism is like saying you favor justice but not oppression in the name of justice. Opposing capitalism in the name of opposing oppression is like opposing abolitionists because you don't like slavery—it makes no sense.

The United States of America are the first nation founded on the principle that all people are created equal. Capitalism is only opposed by those who deny that all people are created equal. In the United States, these are mostly Democrats.

------

1. https://www.newsweek.com/lefts-disgraceful-failure-condemn-cubas-communist-dictatorship-opinion-1610297
2. Watch for my forthcoming book, *Is Socialism Christian?*
3. Mike Gonzalez, "To Destroy America," *City Journal*, September 1, 2020.

10

GREEDY

Democrats, never content, can't get enough of other people's money or property. They simply love to tax and spend, in order to line their own pockets and those of their friends. They are *greedy*. Democrats seem to view private citizens as their own personal piggy bank.

However, plundering the people evenly creates an obvious political problem: The victims will feel the pain and vote for politicians who stop it. Democrats will not be able to continue to pick the pockets of their tax slaves if those slaves vote them out of office. For this reason, Democrats have always pushed for a heavily *progressive* tax structure that leaves at least half of the country with minimal tax burden, while focusing their parasitic desires upon the remaining half, and especially upon the top quarter. The top quarter, they reason, can scream and complain about the injustice all they want; it won't matter to the rest who see that they are getting a pretty sweet deal with others picking up the tab. *Fully 87% of all federal income taxes in the United States are today paid by the top 25% of earners.*[1]

According to the IRS, the top 1% of income earners pay 40% of all federal income taxes, the top 5% pay a whopping 60%, while the bottom 50% of income earners pay only 3%.[2] That is to say, "the rich" in the United States actually pay (on average) *greater than thirteen times more of their income*, in terms of total percentage, than do the *entire* bottom 50% of Americans.

If we wanted everyone to pay their "fair share" of taxes, we would bemoan the fact that half of Americans don't pull their weight in taxes, while top earners are grievously abused. But what do Democrats do? They pretend that the rich are not paying enough, and they grandstand upon demands that the rich be required to cough up even more of the fruits of their efforts. For one hundred years, the United States have had one of the most progressive taxation structures in the world, and this is not a good thing. The U.S. federal tax structure is grossly unjust—especially against those who earn more.

The Federal Income Tax

Income taxes were found unconstitutional by the U.S. Supreme Court in 1895, and it took a constitutional amendment, the 16th (in 1913) to change this fact. The 16th and 17th Amendments have been two of the most damaging to the cause of justice and limitation of tyranny in the United States.

The bottom income tax rate in 1913 was set at 1%, and the top rate at 7%. As such, the income tax was unjust from the very start, since it did not treat rich and poor with an even standard. Income tax rates doubled in 1916, and then tripled again in 1918, with a bottom rate of 6% and a top rate of 77%.

Rates dropped off slightly after World War I, but remained strongly progressive. The top rate reached 94% in 1944. Reagan brought taxes down across the board, and from 1913 to the present day, the fairest the American federal income tax system has been was the period from 1988-1990, when there were only two rates: 15.0% and 28.0%. Sadly, greater injustice soon crept back in.[3]

Other Taxes

Unfortunately, federal income tax accounts for only a portion of an Americans' total tax burden. Americans pay local and state taxes, capital gains taxes, excise taxes (such as gas taxes), property taxes, sales taxes, payroll taxes, Social Security taxes, corporate taxes through higher prices of goods and services that companies must charge in order to cover these additional layers of taxation, and when inheriting they yet again pay taxes on property for which a parent or grandparent already paid taxes in full.

Collecting taxes in these many ways makes it virtually impossible for Americans to even see their own tax burden. A just solution would be to pass a constitutional amendment forbidding taxation of any American at a significantly higher portion of their income than any other, forbidding taxation of owned property (including capital gains), forbidding the estate tax, and requiring that federal tax be collected at only one point—for example, the point of first retail sale of a good or service. The Fair Tax is one proposal that generally follows the pattern I describe here.

What would be the effects? Most importantly, *everyone would feel the burden of taxation* and *everyone would see how much they are paying in tax*. Together, these results would give all Americans "skin in the game," and it would cause *everyone* (not just "the rich") to care about how their federal government is spending money. People would begin to vote very differently. And, they would vote against those who raise taxes and who spend with reckless abandon.

Democrats, of course, who wrongly villify wealth inequality and love to use taxpayers' money against them, would certainly oppose such a move with all their might.

Does Wealth Equal Greed?

Property is a basic principle of justice. "You shall not steal" and "You shall not covet" are two of the Ten Commandments. If ownership of property was not good, then stealing would not be wrong. Jesus did warn against greed (Luke 12:15), and Paul wrote that the love of money is a root of all sorts of evil (I Timothy 6:10). However, these warnings are principally for individuals. The emphasis in the Bible is not upon looking for and punishing greed or the love of money in others, but guarding against it our own hearts.

Some people carelessly associate greed with having or seeking a large income, accumulating much wealth or property, or failing to support or accept socialist redistribution schemes. But while greed could be *present* in any of the above situations, none of these circumstances or attitudes is, on its own, unjust or greedy. Having more wealth does not make you a bad person. Job was said by God himself to be a man who "feared God and turned from evil," (Job 1:1) even while he was also the wealthiest man of all the east (Job 1:3). No, being wealthy or seeking prosperity does not make one greedy.

People often misdirect their anger because they harbor

misconceptions. Truth must always precede justice. As was discussed in Chapter 8, Democrats have a warped sense of justice that includes a belief in involuntary servitude. This is why Democrats pushed the 16th Amendment, and it is why they have insisted upon a system of "progressive" taxation in which some citizens are enslaved to others against their will and essentially without recourse since greater than half of their fellow citizens are simply not experiencing the same abuse. Once the barrier against slavery has been breached— as it was in 1913, just shy of 50 years after passage of the 13th Amendment outlawed involuntary servitude—it is very difficult to rein things back in.

The Politics of Greed

Drawing the topic full circle, we can plainly see that Democrats encourage greed in their voters, telling them that they are victims of the evil rich people who don't pay their "fair share" —even as many of these same voters are already plundering those very people by receiving welfare or housing or phones or subsidized healthcare funded by tax revenues extracted from these top earners.

It is not that having the things needed for life is bad. Greed is lack of contentment, a coveting and spiteful heart, and willingness to perpetrate injustice against others in order to get something for yourself. The Democratic strategy, sadly, rests upon feeding all these wrongs, and (as is the case with any widespread injustice) it has a corrosive and spiraling negative effect over time upon American society, killing productivity and feeding resentment in all directions. Sadly, it does not even really help those who are receiving the lighter burden or the redistributed wealth, but rather (as discussed in Chapter 8) keeps many in a perpetual cycle of bondage and dependence.

———————————————

1. "In 1 Chart, How Much the Rich Pay In Taxes," Heritage Foundation, March 3, 2021.
2. Ibid.
3. "Historical U.S. Federal Individual Income Tax Rates & Brackets, 1862-2021," Tax Foundation, August 24, 2021.

11

DISENFRANCHISERS

Democrats and their allies violated every United States citizen in 2020, and they are ready to do it again in 2024. This statement is not hyperbole or conjecture; it is a plain fact that is well documented in my book *By The People?*

One need not look far into Democrat advocacy efforts on election policy and election law to find a dreadful pattern of support for disenfranchising voters. At every turn, Democrats work to implement practices that rob the votes of citizens. If your vote does not count because someone else voted twice (canceling yours) or voted when they were not eligible to vote (canceling yours or reducing its impact), you have been disenfranchised. You had a right to a full voice, but yours has been silenced. To look at Democrats, you would have to conclude that such a situation brings them sheer joy.

There are many ways your vote can be taken from you. Democrats often reference the very real Jim Crow era abuse —by some parties in the United States—of poll taxes, literacy tests and other ploys to disadvantage political opponents.

Democrats usually neglect to mention that they were the ones pushing, using, and defending such unjust tactics. These Democrat tactics of the past are today recognized by nearly everyone to have been unjust and wrong.

But keeping us from the polls is not the only way that our voices can be silenced, and Democrats know this very well. In fact, they have by now transformed other means of voter disenfranchisement into a well-tuned science, a machine that year after year turns our elections far more to the Democrats' advantage than they would be if the contests were honest. Here are some ways your vote can be (and often is) stolen from you.

1. Someone else votes twice (or more), or their vote is counted twice (or more).

2. Someone (such as a non-citizen) who has no right to vote casts a ballot, and that vote is counted.

3. Corrupt political partisans inside the election system take advantage of weak points in chain-of-custody or other vulnerabilities to change vote counts, discard legitimate votes, or add illegitimate votes.

4. Agents of a political party or campaign target people who can be pressured or manipulated into casting a ballot for a candidate by (for example) "helping" nursing home residents vote and/or "helping" by mailing or delivering those ballots to election officials (but "forgetting" to follow through on the delivery of any ballots not cast for the candidate of choice) or paying people in housing projects for uncast ballots or for a particular vote.

5. Corrupt individuals in government—but outside of the state legislatures who are the only ones constitutionally permitted to set election law— change the times or manners of elections in such a way as to make it easier to cheat and allow votes (such as those cast after election day, those without postmarks, or those without valid signatures) to be counted that have no right to be counted.

These are just a few examples that actually happen today, but it is not an exhaustive list. All such actions, and others like them, cancel or reduce your vote. When we look at Democrat advocacy related to elections and voting processes, the consistent pattern is that the DNC and Democrat operatives almost always support the things that enable the above actions—and almost always oppose (sometimes fiercely) even the most sensible steps to prevent such voter disenfranchisement.

The Totalitarian Mindset

Everyone in politics wants to be known as "for the people." That's because—at least in the United States and other parts of the world living in the heritage of the Enlightenment—it is almost universally understood that representative self-government (that is, rule by the people) is a good thing. But, the spirit of the petty dictator has not disappeared from our world, and it probably never will. Rather, it moves underground, and from there it lurks and operates in the shadows.

Subverting the actual will of the people via manipulation of elections and voter disenfranchisement is the act of petty dictators who do not truly believe the will of the people is all that important. Sure, these dictators will *say* they support "democracy" and elections, but in the end they want those things just for show. The appearance of having won an election is useful because it lends an air of legitimacy to the one who has been "elected." Elected officials in a functional democracy or democratic republic are an extension of the will of the people. This is very different from being an autocrat—one who rules as a result of sheer will, brute force, or corruption. Democrats today, or many of them at least, have the spirit of autocrats. They believe that they know what is best for the people far better than the people themselves know and that if they could just get into power and implement their plans and policies, everyone would soon see what fools they were for ever doubting the superior wisdom of these enlightened leaders.

Because Democrats (and, to be fair, this sort of thinking is not limited to Democrats, though it is most prevalent on the political left today) believe this way, such thinking becomes the basis for an end-justifies-the-means way of operating in the world, and in particular in elections. This is probably why they, while trying not to get caught, work so hard to preserve corrupt election systems that they can manipulate to engineer their own greater electoral success by brute force.

No matter the reason, it is wrong. The problem with such thinking is that every petty dictator in the history of the world has thought exactly the same way. Everyone believes that they know best and that "if only" they were king, then everything would be set right in the world. History has taught, however, that those most hungry for power are often those most willing to bend or discard the rules in order to obtain it and, importantly, also those least qualified to hold it.

The logic of self-governance is that it systematically *trusts* the will of the people. Does a system of truly honest and secure elections ensure that poor representatives will never convince the people and get elected? Absolutely not! But in the big picture, this is likely to happen far less frequently than in other systems because on the balance people have a certain collective wisdom (also tempered by self-interest in such things as goodness and integrity) that is difficult to quantify but that seems to be borne out in well-functioning systems of self-governance.

One major difference between Democrats and Republicans, or (if you will) American leftists and American conservatives today, is that the former tend to embody the elitist mindset while the latter tend to trust the will of the people. This should be noted and understood. I do not trust people who don't listen and who seem to feel that they know it all ... and who because of this try to impose their will by force. How about you?

False Accusations Serving Bad Policy

Again and again, Democrats say that election integrity efforts by Republicans or conservatives—like voter ID laws—are attempts to return to Jim Crow or to suppress votes.[1] But in order to make this assertion, they must insult your intelligence and count on you not being smart enough to understand that, first, identifying the person voting is key to making sure your vote actually counts, and second, not identifying the person voting opens the door for the exploitation of all of the other disenfranchisement opportunities such as those listed above. If U.S. citizens are being denied the right to cast their votes alongside their fellow Americans, I think we can all agree that it should be addressed immediately. I as a conservative American will absolutely join the cause of making sure every citizen eligible to vote has the fair opportunity to do so. But what I will always oppose is the corruption of our elections and disenfranchisement of all U.S. citizens by those who would cast or count illegitimate votes.

---

1. Vazquez, Meagan and Kate Sullivan, "Biden calls Georgia law 'Jim Crow in the 21st Century' and says Justice Department is 'taking a look,'" *CNN*, March 26, 2021. https://www.cnn.com/2021/03/26/politics/joe-biden-georgia-voting-rights-bill/index.html; Devega, Chauncey, "The Republicans have dug up Jim Crow's corpse — and now they've married it," *Salon*, October 28, 2021. https://www.salon.com/2021/10/28/the-have-dug-up-jim-crows-corpse--and-now-theyve-married-it/

12

INFANTILIZING

C hildren require special care and protection. An infant needs to be fed, changed, clothed, cleaned, and shielded from danger until physically and mentally capable of doing things for herself or himself, and of navigating the world so as to recognize and avoid obvious dangers. A parent who allows their infant to crawl unsupervised next to a busy street, or wander free in a crowd, is negligent.

But, once a child has grown into adulthood, there is a natural movement toward responsibility for himself or herself and his or her conduct in the world.

As we grow and mature, it is generally healthy and appropriate for us to spread our wings. Despite the discomfort, arguments between parents and children during the teen years are part of our biology, as kids prepare to operate independently. The self-confidence and independence that seems so overdeveloped and frightening to parents (who were once in the same situation!) may be a necessary[1] push to test and confirm the skills that will one day soon be needed to live without reliance upon the nest in which they were until then nurtured.

So, it is normal to grow up. And, in similar fashion, as grownups we should be able to live without overbearing helicopter-parenting from our government. Independence is a foundational principle of Americanism. There was something wrong with adults being treated as children by the British, and the American colonies fought for self-governance even as they sought to devise a system of government that would prevent unrestrained rule by tyrants that had been materialized under the governing system they were rebelling against.

In essence, being American means affirming the God-given right of people to be free, and to govern themselves. Since we can't do everything entirely on our own—for example, we all need an effective national defense—we require a system for keeping those who govern us under our control. To this end, we elect representatives to be our temporary servants. Our representatives are not our kings, and our government does not rule over us. As citizens, we rule our representatives, giving them a certain limited authority to do business on our behalf and within particular parameters.

This model of governance contrasts with many others throughout human history and even today. In the United States as established, grown-ups are treated as grown-ups.

Treating People Like Children

"Infantilizing" means artificially keeping someone in an infantile state, treating or regarding an otherwise competent individual as a child who is incapable of caring for themselves or taking their place among the society of adults. For an adult to be infantilized is an insult. It may also be an injustice.

People who infantilize others do so for various reasons. First, there are the common motivations of money, sex, and power. Diminishing others is a way to foster a master-servant relationship. A relationship of dependence and subservience is useful for politicians or political leaders in a position to be seen as the ones providing for the safety or needs of the person or people whom they are infantilizing. Once someone believes that they can't survive on their own, it opens the door for politician X or political party Y to swoop in as the savior. Such a politician or political party has gained an advantage over competitors who, either through principle (e.g., a refusal to similarly engage in the practice of infantilizing competent adults) or lack of ability (e.g., not having a fulfillment mechanism to deliver the goods), do not provide the things needed or wanted.

Second, infantilization is habit. If people are conditioned to accept that certain things are the responsibility of government, many just come to accept their subservience. In much of the world, people view government as a parent rather than as a child. As a matter of fact, this feature is one that makes the United States special. Here, the people are the parent, and the government is the child who must be hemmed in, given certain permissions and parameters, and told what it can and cannot do.

Unfortunately, Democrats don't tend to see things that way. I think this is partly because Democrats fundamentally look down on others, considering themselves to be smarter and more enlightened. But, the infantilization of others also serves to advance Democrats' base political and personal interests.

Democrats Infantilize

I have noticed that Democrats tend to treat everyone like children. However, their condescension to some groups is often even more pronounced.

Democrats often act and speak as if they own the nation's women. Famously during debates over Obamacare, Democrats told women that if they do not have contraception paid for by others, they have been abused. Many people saw this message as a multi-layered insult. Are women incapable of making their own decisions with their bodies? Are women all to be assumed as needing contraception? Are women incapable of buying things that they may want or need, just like anyone else might do? Ultimately, Democrats' message to women appeared to be, "You cannot control yourself. You need us to provide for you."

Democrats infantilize minority populations. They seem to say, "You cannot control yourself. We know that you are morally incapable of operating as an adult member of society. You need a different set of rules, and you need us to look out for you. Vote Democrat, and we will make sure you have all kinds of things, including quotas in hiring and admissions, because we Democrats know that you are incapable of making it into college or a job based upon your hard work, personal character, and merits. Those mean old Republicans (shame on them) want to treat you the same as everyone else. Not us Democrats. We are going to lower standards because we are white supremacists who know you are racially inferior and need an extra boost from us if you are going to make it." It is incredibly insulting to members of such groups.

Democrats infantilize Muslims. They seem to say, "We Democrats understand your plight. While most other people can control their reactions, we understand that you are not most other people. You Muslims have no way of controlling your anger when someone offends you. If you happen to fly into a violent rage over something that someone has said, that is not your fault—it is theirs! They should have known better than to offend someone as incapable of living in a grown-up society as yourselves." It is incredibly insulting to Muslims. In contrast, grown adults understand that everyone, including people who believe that Muhammad was a prophet, is capable of making the choice to live as a good neighbor and to control their reactions.

Democrats tell illegal immigrants that they are morally inferior and incapable of following the same laws as everyone else. And then, Democrats blame Republicans for wanting to treat them as adults. "Don't worry," Democrats seem to say, "We Democrats have you covered. We know you are morally inferior. We certainly will not hold you to the same standard that might apply to others. Don't worry about following all those grown-up rules and laws. Those are for mature adults, but we Democrats have a special 'kids eat free' menu for you to choose from. And, here are some crayons for you to color the picture on the back of your menu while you wait for us to bring you your dinner." It is quite insulting.

Democrats tell college students that—even though they are old enough to vote, drive, and get an abortion—the Democrats consider them stupid children who have no ability to understand the concept of taking out a college loan and promising to pay it back later.

Democrats tell "black" voters that they are not capable of bringing an ID to the polling location. It is incredibly insulting, and yet another sign of Democrat hubris and condescension.

I believe that Democrats' tendency to infantilize people as a means of control is reflective of a general habit of viewing other people as mere tools to be used when convenient, and discarded when no longer needed. Once again, such an attitude would be consistent with a naturalist view of the world, one that recognizes no higher moral law than societal consensus and that sees people as mere animals. There could be other causes as well, such as a general abusive tendency of the sort that is commonly seen in people who have themselves been abused by others. Whatever the root cause, I assert that there is a strong correlation between infantilizing behavior and alignment with the Democratic party.

---

1. Necessary does not mean that a parent pushing back and continuing to offer guidance and warning against danger during teen years isn't also necessary or appropriate. Parents should not abandon their kids at the very stage of their lives when their confidence is much larger than their competence. Then need help bring the latter to maturity even while they solidify and take full ownership fo the former.

13

VIOLENT

In Democrat-led Portland, Oregon, on Saturday, August 30, 2020, 48-year-old Antifa supporter Michael Forest Reinoehl allegedly shot and killed Aaron Danielson, a Trump supporter who was wearing the cap of the libertarian-leaning group Patriot Prayer. Soon after, a woman shouted into a megaphone at a nearby BLM-Antifa gathering, "I am not sad that a f-king fascist died tonight." An American flag was burned in celebration.[1] On June 16, Reinoehl said in a social media post, "Every revolution needs people that are willing and ready to fight...I am 100 % ANTIFA all the way! I am willing to fight for my brothers and sisters!...We do not want violence but we will not run from it either!...Today's protesters and antifa are my brothers in arms."[2]

Democratic presidential nominee Joe Biden, the following day, said in a statement, "we must not become a country that accepts the killing of fellow Americans who do not agree with you," but later seemed to blame President Trump for the alleged actions of the BLM-Antifa supporter: "What does President Trump think will happen when he continues to insist on fanning the flames of hate and division in our society and using the politics of fear to whip up his supporters."[3]

Blaming the victims is a common tactic of murderers, bullies, and those who support them. Democrats quite frequently fall into one or more of these three categories.

In June of 2017, Anti-Trump Bernie Sanders supporter James Hodgkinson opened fire upon a congressional baseball game, letting off more than fifty shots and taking down Republican Congressman Steve Scalese who was taken to the hospital in critical condition.

DC-area radio host Chris Plante has said (I paraphrase from memory), "If Democrats would stop shooting people, 90% of gun crime would disappear." The statement was made with rhetorical flair and not scientific precision, but its general assertion is probably correct.

Democrats Support Terrorism

Terrorism is an act of violence perpetrated to achieve a social or political purpose. When a playground bully beats up those who approach the swingset, he is a terrorist. He wants everyone watching to see and "decide" not to go near the swingset. Terrorism is essentially conditioning people to behave the way you want by a credible threat of harm if they do not. It is essentially a tantrum thrown by someone who cannot make a reasoned argument for their position.

Terrorism continues when it gets rewarded. If everyone on the playground stays away from the swingset (even though they have a perfect right to use it), then the terrorism has been successful and will continue or even increase.

Terrorism is a central part of Democrat tactics today.

They love to give terrorists cover when those people are doing their bidding. We see it in cancel culture and the shaming and firing of CEOs or other individuals in companies who commit some "sin" against wokeness.

When transgender Audrey Hale walked into a school in Nashville and shot to death three children and three adult staff, the Biden White House issued statement delivered by Press Secretary Karin Jean Pierre, seeming to support the shooter and blame the victims. Video captured and posted by Chicks On the Right showed supporters saying they don't blame Hale; they blame the gun. This would, of course, be akin to saying, "Don't blame Hitler, blame the gas chambers," or "Don't blame Jeffrey Dahmer, blame the Black & Decker drill," or "Don't blame the 19 men for 9/11, blame the airplanes." Like terrorist supporters, Madonna blamed the victims, saying, "Anyone with half a brain knows not to (mess) with a drag queen."[4]

Policies That Lead To Violence

In earlier chapters, we discussed the fact that gun control leads to an increase in the number and severity of victimization crimes, including violent crimes. Gun control, in particular, leads to murder and mass shooting on a greatly increased scale as the deterrrent value of armed law-abiding citizens is removed from the picture. Other factors leading to increased violence have included Democrat pushes for "restorative justice," which curtails punishment for violent crimes. The sentiment is not always bad, but the results of "restorative justice" have often been tragic, as more innocent people are victimized by the recipients of Democrat compassion. In the bigger picture, Democrat billionaire George Soros has been active in securing the election of activists into the judicial system who are working toward widespread release of people duly convicted of crimes, and lenience toward those facing conviction. The failure to have serious penalties for crimes, however, leads to a breakdown of society and a great expansion in the number of victims. It is not justice.

Going To Any Length To Excuse Perpetrators

It would be hilarious if it weren't so serious. The New York Times tweet on September 11, 2019 read, "18 years have passed since airplanes took aim and brought down the World Trade Center." Yes, you read that right: airplanes took aim. The New York Times was rightly ridiculed for its tweet, and forced to take it down.[5] However, their deflection of blame from the *people who do evil* follows a clear and common pattern by Democrats. For them, it is always the fault of someone other than the criminal.

1. Miranda Devine, "BLM 'activists' celebrated as Trump supporter was killed: Devine," *New York Post,* August 30, 2020, https://nypost.com/2020/08/30/blm-activists-celebrated-as-trump-supporter-killed-devine/.
2. Mairead McCardle, "Portland Shooter Declared Allegiance to Antifa, Was Previously Arrested for Bringing Gun to Protest," *National Review,* August 31, 2020, https://www.nationalreview.com/news/portland-shooter-declared-allegiance-to-antifa-was-previously-arrested-for-bringing-gun-to-protest/
3. M. Devine, *op. cit.*
4. Dave Paulson, "Madonna slams Tennessee laws on drag shows, gender-affirming care: 'Unfounded and pathetic'", *Nashville Tennesseean*, March 28, 2023.
5. Ashley Kimber, "Blame The Gun, Blame The Airplane – NYT Deletes Its Embarrassingly Bad 9/11 Take," *Chicks On The Right*, September 11, 2019.

14

HATEFUL

The old bumper sticker reads "Hate is not a family value." In truth, there is nothing wrong with hate when directed against evil things. The Bible associates hate with sincere love: "Love must be sincere. Hate what is evil, cling to what is good" (Roman 12:9). It is appropriate to hate injustice, to hate cruelty and abuse, to hate theft and fraud, and to hate the victimization of the innocent. But hate should be directed against things, not against people. For one person to hate another is short-sighted at best.

Whether directed toward ideas (such as an uncomfortable truth, or a vicious and destructive falsehood) or situations (such as injustice) or a person, hate is an emotion that comes and goes. There are people who have a great deal of hatred in their hearts; sometimes it is there because they have been wounded, sometimes it is because they have a strong and properly calibrated sense of justice that takes up causes left and right, and sometimes it is caused by a misguided set of assumptions about the world that leads the person to lash out when doing so is not justified.

And, as was the case with some of the other chapters, there are examples of people who are hateful and unkind on all sides. Also, people can consider things to be hateful that really are not. Telling someone a truth that they may not want to hear can be a very loving act, but it can be seen as hate by the recipient or even by others. For all these reasons, and also because space is short, I will not list examples but rather make some general observations from my own vantage point and experience.

General Observations

First, and this might surprise readers who by this point in the book are expecting a universal negative assessment of everything related to Democrats, I have observed and experienced that there are a lot of Democrats who are very kind, gentle, loving, and generous individuals. I have known Democrats over the years who are very thoughtful toward others, very welcoming of strangers, and who are among the first to make a person from another culture or background feel welcome.

All of the foregoing are commendable. I hope that such people, when they read this book, would become moved to reconsider their alignments.

Now, to the point. I have been very active on social media for about as long as it has existed. I treat Facebook and Twitter like a glorified coffee shop, where I can have conversations with all kinds of people, friends, acquaintances, even complete strangers. I love the venue for the opportunity to meet new people and to have interesting and important conversations—and the best of these are with those who disagree strongly.

I am not shy about discussing any topic about which I have knowledge, but I am not unkind. I love passionate discussions. They keep me sharp and feel purposeful. Aware that people cannot hear tone of voice over a typed message, I make a point to interject from time to time during a heated discussion how much I love and appreciate my friend on the other side, and I thank them. I do this also for the sake of people sitting on the sidelines, so that they can understand that we do not dislike each other. I have *never* blocked or unfriended *anyone*. And this brings me around the long way to my first point: I have indeed been unfriended by a number of Democrat friends over the years, and the unfriending has happened not because I was unkind, but *because they did not like my positions*.

Mind you, I was not chasing after them, stalking them, or hounding them. I was engaging very respectfully in public discussion, often in which many others were also taking part. My observation is that, in almost every case, my contributions to the discussions were just making them look bad by showing up the flaws in their positions, until in anger they shut me out. But of course it is disappointing when such a thing happens at the hands of people who you know, and until then respected, in the real world.

Bitter Fruit

For most of the history of our nation, the phrase, "I don't agree with what you say, but I will defend to the death your right to say it," was emblematic of American civil discourse in the shadow of the First Amendment.

For me, the most concerning manifestation of hate is the one that justifies violence and even calls for the death of those who disagree. Such has emerged among the left, from Democrats, after about 2015. This is serious business, since the left is also sympathetic to Marxism and socialism, and we know the history of the two great proponents of those ideologies (Lenin and Hitler) in dealing with those in their societies that they judged politically inconvenient.

On July 15, 2021, Fairfax, Virginia NAACP leader Michelle Leete spoke at a public protest at the Thomas Jefferson High School for Science and Technology. Her remarks were directed against parents and other citizens who had voiced objections to the teaching or implementation of the principles of marxist Critical Race Theory in Loudoun County Public schools. She said:

> So let's meet and remain steadfast in speaking truth, tearing down double standards, and refuting double talk. Let's not allow any double downing on lies. Let's prepare our children for a world they deserve. Let's deny this off-key band of people that are anti-education, anti-teacher, anti-equity, anti-history, anti-racial reckoning, anti-opportunities, anti-help people, anti-diversity, anti-platform, anti-science, anti-change agent, anti-social justice, anti-healthcare, anti-worker, anti-LGBTQ+, anti-children, anti-healthcare, anti-worker, anti-environment, anti-admissions policy change, anti-inclusion, anti-live-and-let-live people. **Let them die.**[1]

---

1. Bacon, James. "Let Them Die," *The Bull Elephant,* July 17, 2021. (emphasis added)

15

IRRATIONAL

One of the effects of hate is a dulling of the rational faculties. In recent years, the American left has descended further and further into incoherence. Whatever the cause, and I do believe it is a combination of factors among which hate figures prominently, the Democrat Party is unquestionably mired in contradictions. A hardcore Democrat will state in one breath that we should not legislate morality, after all "love is love," that truth is relative and a biblical worldview is oppressive and patriarchal—they will ridicule Mike Pence for maintaining a personal policy of not being in a room alone with a woman other than his wife. Then, in the very next breath, the same Democrat will condemn the sexual predations of Harvey Weinstein or Jeffrey Epstein. Why? If truth is relative and there is no real standard of right and wrong, by what token can anyone say that what these men did to their victims is actually wrong?

I know the answer, because I believe there is an objective moral standard, but Democrats are often incoherent and arbitrary on such things.

Ultimately, Democrats are caught in a postmodern trap. They want to take a moral stance when doing so serves their own interests, but they lack any moral authority since they insist that truth does not exist in the first place. They have pulled the rug from under themselves. It is funny to watch but also quite serious because of the grave consequences.

Much has been mentioned in preceding chapters and there is a need here only to give a few more examples. You can fill in the rest from your own personal experiences and observation.

Endless Contradiction

"Rape is wrong," Democrats say. But then they insist that truth is relative. If Democrats believe truth is relative, how can they say that Jeffrey Epstein's actions were wrong? Wasn't he just "living his truth"?

"Believe all women," Democrats say. But then they insist, "We don't know what a woman is."

Could Joe Biden make history as the first woman president by self-identifying as such for one day while holding office? Under their absurd ideology of truth being whatever someone says it is, Democrats would be forced to accept it.

But wait: People can self-identify as a woman or man, or even as another *species*, but no one can self-identify as another race. Why not? What is the rationale for this arbitrary constraint on which portions of reality are open to fluidity and which are not?

And, these are just a few of the corners that Democrats have painted themselves into. Ultimately, the point is that most of their arguments are mere sophistry, a pretext to do whatever they feel like doing.

PART II

DISCUSSION

16

RED IS DEMOCRAT, BLUE IS REPUBLICAN

Did you know that the Republican Party is the Blue party, and the Democrats are the Red? It's true! Until the mid-1980s, political maps in the United States were most frequently printed with Democrat states or areas colored red, and Republican ones blue.

Then, in the late 1980s, U.S. media elites and others seem to have agreed to switch the colors to red for Republicans and blue for Democrats. I believe that the change was not benign, but was carried out with an intent to deceive. And, I argue that the colors should be switched back.

Does it matter which of the two colors represents each party? Absolutely! Red and blue have taken on worldwide meanings in relation to politics that will be discussed below. Also, these two colors subconsciously stir different emotions and sentiments.

The association of red with Democrats and blue with Republicans before the final decade of the 20th Century affects both how we perceive the present and how we remember the past. In the minds of people who were born in

the 1970s or prior, blue signifies—among other things—
opposition to slavery, support for Civil Rights legislation,
opposition to racism and bigotry and injustice.

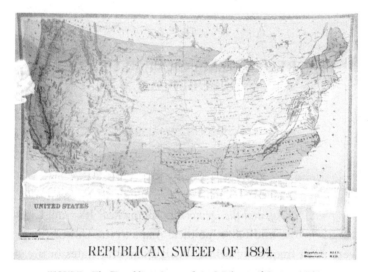

FIGURE 1: The "Republican Sweep of 1894" (Library of Congress) This
map, of the result of the 1894 election, in which Republicans won 253
seats, compared with just 93 for Democrats. Though not shown in color in
the main edition of this book, this map depicts the southern states of
Texas, New Mexico, Louisiana, Arkansas, Louisiana, Mississippi,
Alabama, Georgia, South Carolina, Florida, Virginia, Maryland, and
Kentucky, controlled by the Democrats in red. All other states, where
Republicans were victorious, are shown in blue.

Flipping the party associations to red for Republican and
blue for Democrat was, I believe, a maneuver favored by
many on the American and global Left who wanted to get
ordinary Americans to remember the past differently by
inferring a link between today's Republicans and yesterday's
Democrats. They especially wanted—indeed, *needed*—to
help current Democrats escape accountability to their own

past without requiring them abandon their own principles, to which they remain deeply committed to this day.

There is more to consider, certainly, than merely the historic American associations for these colors; red and blue also have different psychological effects on people. Generally, blue gives an impression of intelligence, thoughtfulness, and trustworthiness. It is also the *favorite* color of more people in the world than any other. Red, on the other hand, while associated with attractiveness, energy, and strength, also suggests aggressiveness, impulsiveness, and anger.

It is worth noting that modern political convention has typically associated blue with more conservative or thoughtful parties or movements, and red with more radical or revolutionary ones. Such symbolism in the latter instance aligns well with the sense of energy, aggressiveness, and perhaps impetuousness ("act now and don't ask questions") that characterizes the radicals.

And finally, red has long been used to signify Communist movements worldwide. I believe this association is the main reason the American Democrat Party to be the true and proper red party in the United States. Democrats' open advocacy of socialism and (though not yet openly in the higher offices) growing sympathy for Communism is today evident to all.

Political parties are vehicles enabling people to align around certain moral convictions and philosophies to better advance them through the strength that comes from association. Like any human organization, a party may remain generally true to its founding principles, or it may drift. Drift is common. For example, many of the Ivy League universities in the United States today were founded with a very Christian ethos that also embraced the free inquiry that is the heart of any academic endeavor—yet these are in major part today hostile to these founding sentiments and hostile to free thought and free speech.

The fact that organizations can drift over time does not mean they always do. My argument in this book has been that both the Republican and Democrat parties in the United States have remained substantially true to their core principles over the course of their existence, altering only their façades as social changes in the United States and the world have come to pass.

The Republican Party is the party of liberty and justice for all, of recognition that a moral law exists, of appreciation for and curiosity about the world as it actually is, of grace and love and a hope for all humans to have the best possible range of opportunities in the midst of life's unexpected blessings and hardships.

The Democrat Party is the party of utopia in which some serve others against their will, immorality and self-righteousness, division and racism and ever increasing social stratification, of hate and violence enabled by embrace of the religion of moral relativism, shared misery for the majority and unassailable opulence for the elites and their friends.

17

WHAT'S REALLY WRONG

"The biggest political party in this country, which is the Democrat Party...is the Fifth Column. It is the cancer on the body politic...It is! **When you have a party that has as its mission turning over the institutions, the belief systems, the values, the structures of the country, turning the culture inside-out–not for persuasion of the citizenry, but [for] changing the citizenry–well then, you have a political party that's more dangerous than any foreign enemy we have**...Our greatest threat today is not a foreign power...the rot from within...is promoted by the Democrat Party."

— MARK LEVIN, MAY 10, 2018

W hy do Democrats insist upon accusing Republicans and conservatives of many of the flaws that form the subjects of the preceding chapters of this book? Is it because Republicans are actually guilty of them also? In fact, it could be (and almost certainly is) true that *particular* Republicans exhibit some of these traits. But the real test would surely be whether the Republican Party embraces these things in principle by either active affirmation or passive assent. Does it?

In fact, the Republican Party does not. What Democrats are doing when they accuse others of all these things has a name in clinical psychology: Projection (or, alternately, Transference). At a personal level, this means that people are deeply aware of their most prominent personal flaws but are unwilling to face their reality and so try to deflect attention from their shame by loudly accusing others of the very same things.

But Why Are Democrats Like This?

Ideas and moral principles have consequences, and when you see a person or group of people acting in an internally logical or coherent way, it is foolish to think that the 1) goals and 2) ways chosen from a range of options to reach those goals–are not influenced by the person's guiding principles and deeply held core beliefs. Goals represent aspirations and can be driven by self interest or by a vision of what the world *should* be like: "The world would be a better place if (X)." People may have different goals. One child wants to be a firefighter and another a businessperson.

Some goals may be driven by a sense of duty or moral obligation. Not all goals driven by a sense of moral duty, however, are good. The nineteen men who hijacked and flew planes into buildings on September 11 did so in pursuit of an ideology.

Since evil ideas can have such dreadful consequences, we must take ideas seriously, and do our best to be on the side of what is good and not on the side of what is evil. There is a divide in American culture today at precisely this point. Some Americans espouse multiculturalism–which makes the (absurd on its face) assertion that there is no truth, but rather that truth—including moral truth—may be different for different people. Such people claim that whatever they call truth is merely a matter of preference; thus they use terms like "my truth" and "your truth." These Americans mostly fall on the American left, the 'progressive' side of the spectrum, and tend to vote for the Red Democrat Party.

Other Americans recognize that truth—including moral truth—does exist and can be discovered or discerned, even if imperfectly. They tend to fall on the American right, the 'conservative' side of the spectrum, and tend to vote for the Blue Republican Party.

The latter sentiment, that truth exists, is foundational of the United States of America. Without it, the United States are just an accident of history and nothing of substance whatsoever. For, how can it be asserted that certain truths are "self evident" and certain rights have been "endowed" by our "Creator" and are therefore "unalienable" if neither Creator nor Truth exist? How can it be asserted that the pedophile or rapist is any worse, objectively, than that of those who would stop them or call them to account, if there is no such thing as truth and their actions are based upon equal footing with all others?

The United States, if anything, are a nation of laws. But these laws rest upon certain non-negotiable premises, the great truths that were not created by the Founders but recognized by them and by others before and since.

If You Are A Democrat

A Democratic Party that rejects racism, stands against immorality, abhors violent rhetoric and action, embraces justice and equality, advocates love of others instead of hate and division and envy, follows science wherever it leads, sets policy based upon true compassion, acts humbly and reflectively rather than in a frenzy of self-righteous fury, does not seek to dictate every detail of everyone's life, and no longer acts like an abusive spouse toward citizens and taxpayers would look very different from the Party as it exists of today.

Will you stand up and try to correct these things in your own back yard? If you find the party will not budge or abandon its commitment to flawed principles, will you leave?

If You Are A Republican

Will you please stop accepting the Democrat narrative about you and about themselves? Use your own language and use it accurately. You are the party of compassion, of justice, of goodness, of liberty. You are the party that makes a way for people at *any* starting point to see a light at the end of the tunnel. You are the party that embraces the truth of science and is willing to follow it wherever it leads. You are the party that understands that upholding and lauding a moral standard is good for everyone even if not followed by everyone. And you are the party that treats people as people and understands that there is no need to hyphenate. Embrace it. Take pride in it. And encourage your more sluggish and entrenched colleagues and representatives who have internalized the left's false characterization of Republicans to wake up and re-acquaint themselves with their identity.

18

COMMUNISM'S DREADFUL RECORD

Communism has been tried many times over a period of hundreds of years, and even in the early American colonies. During the late 1800s, Karl Marx, a Manchester malcontent with sloppy reasoning, dusted off this ancient tyranny and made it fashionable again. Marx encouraged people to covet their neighbors, fanned the flames of hatred and division toward full-scale zealous implementation of Communism in country after country over the past one hundred years. In every instance, it failed to fulfil its promises while causing widespread misery and injustice, and also in most cases the outright murder of countless innocents.

Victims of Communism, whose blood and tears cry out, are owed a public accounting of its record lest its evils be repeated and multiplied.[1] Since the overarching theme of this book is that the Democratic Party is playing with Communism, let us conclude on this note, with sincere hope that the Democrats change course.

Like every other bad ideology, Communism fails because

it rests upon false premises. Communism fails more spectacularly and universally than other bad ideologies because of the magnitude, number, and nature of its errors. Among them:

- False premise #1: God does not exist
- False premise #2: unequal wealth is inherently unjust
- False premise #3: involuntary servitude is alright
- False premise #4: dissent should be forcibly suppressed
- False premise #5: murder is justifiable
- False premise #6: checks and balances are unnecessary
- False premise #7: the laws of economics can be ignored
- False premise #8: the Party is always right

Although this book covers more than the marxist worldview, it is centrally concerned with the fact that marxist premises are increasingly animating the Democratic Party in the United States.

---

1. More than 100 million killed, billions more held in bondage. https://victimsofcommunism.org

GLOSSARY

autocrat (n.) A person who seizes political power against the will of the governed.

capitalism (n.) An economic system aligning with biblical principles of justice, specifically, 1) people have a moral right to their bodies and to their lives that is justly overridden without their consent only by God, and 2) property acquired through labor or trade or gift is the tangible residue of life, and therefore the right of the person who so acquired it. Capitalism requires the honoring of private contracts freely entered into. Although all people of any belief may participate productively in capitalism, its core assertions and its defense rest upon the existence of a moral law, which premise rests upon the existence of God. Capitalism does not permit people to be held involuntary servitude.

chattel slavery (n.) Involuntary servitude, with the one enslaved treated as property of the enslaver.

Communism (n.) A radical materialist political system under which all property is owned and distributed by the state. Modern Communism is rooted in the writings of Marx and Engels (see *marxism*). Communism dogmatically denies the existence of God, and therefore also denies the existence of human rights.

fascism (n.) A totalitarian materialist political ideology that mostly falls on the far-left of the American political spectrum. Fascists favor centralized authoritarian power in the hands of autocrats, maintained by force. Like all totalitarian ideologies, fascists elevate identity groups based upon factors such as race, and suppress individual rights in the name of the "greater good," to be defined, of course, by those in power. Because they devalue the individual, fascists often advocate for suppression of individual property rights, most commonly through the implementation of socialism. Fascists reject all the core principles of the American right: individual liberty, equality of all people before the law, small federal government with enumerated powers (all other powers remaining at state or local level), checks and balances, and self governance with only elected leaders having power to make laws. Those on the left often allege that fascism is a "far-right" ideology, based upon its nationalism. However, autocratic rule, socialism, and unaccountable centralized government—all of which are central to fascism—are directly opposed to the fundamental principles of the American right but defining traits of the American left.

marxism (n.) Political philosophy aligning with or descended from the writings of Karl Marx or Friedrich Engels. The word is capitalized when referring explicitly to Marx's writings or theories. Although his writings were complex, as used in this book, "marxism" mainly signifies an embrace of a dogma that inequity of wealth is unjust, and that people do not have a right to their own labor or its fruits. It is fair to take this short-hand definition because the basic disagreement between leftists and everyone else today (just as at the time of the U.S. Civil War) rests upon differing opinions on whether people are naturally entitled to the fruits of their labors or not. Democrats and marxists argue that they are not. Marxism thus mandates involuntary servitude.

materialism (n.) The belief that there is no reality beyond the physical world.

negative right (n.) A right to not have another person interfere with a particular liberty. A negative right costs another person nothing, and so never infringes anyone else's right. All human rights are negative rights.

totalitarianism (n.) A government in which government exercises absolute power and control.